SOMETHING'S FISHY IN ITALY

A TRAVEL ADVENTURE AND
UNORTHODOX GUIDE
FOR THE CURIOUS TRAVELER

BY

STEVEN A. TENCATI

DEDICATION

TO MY LOVING WIFE, ANOUSH,
WHO IS MY LIFE COMPANION AND BEST FRIEND,
AMD WITHOUT WHOM THESE STORIES WOULD
BE MEANINGLESS AND DEVOID OF JOY.
HER LOVE, LOYALTY, TOLERANCE AND
LAUGHTER HAVE MADE MY LIFE
AND MY TRAVELS
AN EXTRAORDINARY ADVENTURE
AND FOR THAT,
I AM FOREVER GRATEFUL.

TABLE OF CONTENTS

CHAPTER I

Buon Giorno Palermo

We arrived in Palermo in the late morning and as promised our driver was standing at the airport arrival area with a hand lettered sign announcing our name. My bold attempt to greet him in Italian with a hearty "Buon Giorno!" was immediately rewarded with a smile, a nod and a "Come this way" in perfectly accented English. Our bags were balanced precariously one upon another as we wheeled our way across the parking lot to our driver's private car. This turned out to be a small Fiat with just enough space for me, my wife and in the trunk our now forcefully squashed suitcases. My further attempts at conversation were met with more tolerant smiles and very few words either in English or Italian. Our driver, who was chosen by our host, drove through the choked streets with dizzying speed swerving around pedestrians and merely slowing for red lights. The city at this point was a marvelous blur of sounds, sights and people. My excited exclamations of "Look at that!" and "What is this building?" were met with no more than a glance in the rear view mirror and the briefest of explanations, such as, "It's a church." I had been told how warm and welcoming the people of Sicily were but rather than further distract our driver, I decided that his attention was better spent on his navigational prowess and occasional outbursts directed at other drivers. Besides, it was late in the morning and approaching noon on a hot day. I opened the window, sat back and enjoyed the sights whizzing past, a collage of colors and sounds wonderfully foreign to my eyes and ears.

Our driver dropped us off at the entrance to the Capo Market in the center of Palermo and handed us the keys to our rented apartment. He gestured toward the market street, Via Porta Carini, and announced, "It's just there-not far." And with a wave of his hand, we were left with two rolling suitcases, two handbags, a computer carry bag and my wife's over-sized purse at the busy entrance to a market street, now choked with tourists taking pictures, locals buying produce, and the occasional motorcycle driver who apparently believed that this almost pedestrianized street was most suitable for through traffic.

We managed to balance the load and began our walk down Via Porta Carini. The entrance to the market street is wide with competing vegetable sellers on either side. Bright, shiny tomatoes vie for space with zucchini flowers, eggplant of varying sizes, peppers of all colors and fresh fruit. Looking up provides a view of two identical corner buildings with four ancient spires on the ends of each, vaguely moorish in appearance and each decaying in its own charming, old world way. This was not

ning over several toes and pushing some probably very nice people into each other. Via Porta Carini is paved with what look to be ancient, oversized cobblestones not exactly designed for rolling suitcases, and our load continually shifted with the slant of the pavers making the journey much more perilous. Occasionally we had to halt our slow progress to retrieve an errant bag that had decided on its own to try out the cobblestone street rather than enjoy the bumpy ride on its brother's shoulders. When this happened, we were treated to the clicking of tongues and the rolling of eyes that told us we should have planned better. We were in desperate search of number 18, a prearranged vacation rental that promised a view onto what the website declared to be "one of the city's most charming market streets".

The Capo Market is a riot of colors, smells, sights and sounds. An incredible array of fresh produce, fish, meat and spices all contend for space on the narrow street along with Sicilian street food vendors cooking small, garlicky snails, greasy spleen sandwiches, symfonia-a kind of thick bread with a topping of scant tomato sauce and anchovy-and other delectables. Shopkeepers occasionally call out in Sicilian in a sing-song style, tourists take selfies with vegetables and fish, and local residents can be seen buying tomatoes, eggplant and bread and either haggling over the price or simply catching up on the local gossip. On occasion, a group of tourists with no intention of making a purchase are whisked down the street in a throng all taking pictures while a guide holding a closed umbrella aloft states the obvious: "This is one of the busiest market streets in Palermo." They are not wrong, but I have never figured out why one needed a guide to walk a market street. On tables covered with heavy brown paper, baskets of strawberries are neatly laid out next to blueberries, apricots, peaches, grapes, bananas, melons, oranges, and even pineapples. No explanation seems necessary. Hand lettered signs announce the various prices and many items can be had for less than one euro. One seller had two very long tables on which were perched two equally stacked mountains of cauliflower: a riot of yellow, green and white. I was struck with a childish urge to pull one out from the bottom and see what would happened to the mountain, but reason got the better of me. After all, I was new here and not so young as to be forgiven such behavior.

An incredibly large tuna nearly two feet in diameter is proudly displayed and pieces are cut to order. I was reminded of the old pictures I have seen of the annual tuna fishing festival that took place in the seas around Palermo during May and June. It was called the Mattanza. It was a five hundred year old tradition that has largely died out for the lack of tuna in the modern times. Schools of bluefin tuna were herded into nets and bludgeoned to death with wooden cudgels. The ensuing bloodbath was at once gruesome and mesmerizing. After tuna, only the majestic swordfish commands such respect. Indeed, several swordfish heads, deeply embedded in the ice, proud swords pointing skyward greet local and tourist alike. Smaller and more common fish abound along with their smells emanating from every fish vendor's stall.

The Sicilian sun is merciless and unforgiving, especially if you happen to be a dead fish. How long these fish can sit in the sun is anyone's guess. I made a mental note to buy fish only in the early morning hours but soon came to the realization that the fish staring blankly into the afternoon sun would be some of the same fish for sale the next morning. Locals look at the eyes of the fish for freshness. This is an art but even a novice can begin to discern that cloudy eyes and a slight smell of ammonia mean an older fish while clear eyes and the fishy smell of the ocean mean freshness.

No one is offering samples here, too many passing tourist groups. I found that stopping to actually buy a basket of sweet smelling strawberries changed the nature of the encounter with these proud and hard working people. They became solicitous, offered a taste, asked from where we were visiting, smiled broadly and lost any air of intimidation that I had imagined. A few older vendors were somewhat stern and clearly preferred their local customers, but the sons and daughters helping them were warm and friendly. I learned that persistence was the best weapon when trying to win over a vendor. Eventually, everyone takes pity on the poor foreigner desperately trying to understand the money, the weights and measures, and the language.

The heady smell of frying edibles from market stalls mixes with the smells of fresh produce and fish, and finally blends with exhaust fumes pouring from passing motorcycles. These are not the small, cute Vespas seen in quaint village towns, but full sized motorcycles, most with their tailpipes missing. The loud revving noises of the engines being somewhat of a warning of what is approaching from behind. A group of disoriented tourists all try to move to one side or the other to avoid a collision, and then straighten out and move on shaking their heads in amazement. It has always been a mystery to me that many people who have traveled this far would now hesitate to stop, to taste, to smell or to buy from the bounty all around them. Everyone seems intent on capturing the market in freeze frame. Cameras take the place of an actual experience. I imagine that once these camera wielding tourists reach home they will proudly show a photograph of beautiful rows of ripe tomatoes gleaming under the sun. A pity they will not be able to describe the flavor of the fruit, recount the broken conversation with the vendor, describe the confusion of sorting through unfamiliar coins or recall the broad smiles of the Sicilian people striving to make them welcome.

It turned out that our driver's idea of "not far" and our idea of "not far" were very different. After tripping and stumbling down three full blocks of Via Porta Carini, we seemed no nearer to number 18. The left side of the street was announcing numbers in the 70s. I could not find numbers on the right. The market street was ending into a residential area and we were still not there. Turning around at a construction site at the end of the market, I noticed that the numbers on the right were in the 40s while the numbers on the left were in the 60s. I would later come to appreciate that in Sicily, the building addresses began at one on the left side of the street, and simply increase sequentially all on the left: two, three, four and so on, except for the occasional unexplained gap in numbers. At some point, the numbers stop, and the street name changes. On our street, it was at number seventy-five on the left that the numbers stopped. Looking directly across the street would reveal number seventy-six on the right and by backtracking down the street you can, in theory, find seventy-seven, seventy-eight and so on. It was in this way that I learned that number 18 on the right was directly across from 42 on the left. Simple. It didn't really help that the market stalls and the consequent piles of produce boxes and fish crates were stacked in front of the house numbers so that only about every fifth number was visible.

After a few stumbles and re-stacking of the bags we arrived at our apartment just beside a very large outdoor fish market. The canopy of the market stall covered about half of the fish providing a measure of shade and a slightly cooler environment. The balance of the fish glistened in the sun partially covered in rapidly retreating ice. As the ice melted, rivulets of milky looking fishy water escaped between the boxes and quietly made its way to the ruts and crevices in the road. "Peche spade di nostro mare!" was the almost deafening roar of the fish monger as we passed. Indeed, here was another large swordfish head, sword attached, stuck in the ice with the nose turned toward the sky as if saluting our arrival. I smiled and nodded to our official greeter, but the fish just glared at us suspiciously with one un-blinking eye as we passed as if to say, "What are YOU doing here?

My wife at this point in our journey, was laughing hysteri-cally, nearly unable to help move the suitcases. Let me explain. Over the years I have learned that the level of calamity we are facing bears an inverse relationship to the uncontrollable laugh-ter that accompanies me in the form of my wife. Don't get me wrong. Things could be much worse. Her laughter simply re-minds me that my well thought out plans and months of preparations are often not as perfect as I might imagine. I used to get angry thinking she was making fun of my efforts, but now I know better and just wonder how much more laughter I will be hearing in the coming days.

CHAPTER II
An Apartment in Palermo

Our driver had given us a set of three keys to the apartment. I was relieved when the latch on the door of number eighteen actually yielded to the second key I tried and we were able to push past the two motorcycles parked in the narrow stairwell. As I looked around, I realized that none of the pretty pictures on the website included an elevator. I should have known better. This building, I would learn later, was built in 1275. Inside the stairwell was an electrical box at ground level giving out an ominous electrical hum and an occasional click. I decided not to touch it. Looking some 15 feet ahead, I could make out steep stone steps leading to our first floor accommodation. Beyond the eighth step darkness prevailed.

Suddenly, from the darkness above, a young man bounded into view. He clambered down the stairs as sure as a goat on a familiar hillside. I introduced myself in fractured Italian. He smiled, said welcome in perfect English and reached for my wife's bags. Turning, he stopped and pointed to a keypad next to the humming electrical box: "The light is here." A second, smaller key fit the keypad and a quick turn to the right brought the balance of the stairs into view: All twenty-five of them. A straight, steep and narrow passage like a tunnel leading up with no clear destination. As I struggled with my suitcase, he flew past me with one bag aloft and another in tow. He opened the door to our apartment and gave us another of his genuinely welcoming smiles. He turned out to be the son of the owner, who lived up yet another set of stairs.

It is difficult to find the right words for this apartment. Magnificent? Awe-inspiring? Museum quality? All fall short. This was clearly the abode of past nobility, and perhaps more recently a wealthy banker. The rooms were enormous. The entryway had two tables, one on either side with a mirror over the larger one. A chandelier hung from the center of the vaulted ceiling. Each arm of the chandelier was made from casted brass in fantastic curving shapes. The floor was made of contrasting black and white tiles. There were chairs from the eighteenth and nineteenth century placed along the wall. As we entered the living room, we were met by a curved and vaulted ceiling with stucco accents and frescos over its entire surface. It was overwhelming and a bit dizzying. In the center of the room, a piano from 1845 had music carefully laid out on its surface. Texts so old that the yellowed pages were fading. Next to it, a full sized and partially gilded harp from 1620. Persian rugs with Moorish designs adorned the floor. Furniture from another era lined the room—couches and chairs upholstered in the fashion of Louis

XIV. Two narrow balconies on either side of the room gave views over the market street. The walls were covered with old family portraits, etching from some long forgotten artist and an odd mix of post modern paintings. A framed peacock portrait that dominated the wall nearest the balcony turned out to be a fabric woven with gold thread to imitate the sheen of the peacock's plumage in the sun.

Turning right and entering the master bedroom revealed another cavernous room with a vaulted ceiling and a large, full length, impressively ornamented three door armoire for our clothes. At the foot of the bed was a tuck and button upholstered bench. Another magnificent chair and two end tables, all carved and gleaming in dark wood, were against the wall. The headboard and footboard of the bed were similarly carved and polished. I could not resist the urge to immediately lie on the bed thinking that any moment servants would appear to do my bidding. Again, full length French doors led to another narrow balcony that also overlooked the market street.

Forcing myself to continue, I crossed the bedroom and mounted two steps to find a magnificent study, another gilded chandelier, and an enormous bookcase with crosshatch glass and brass doors behind which would be found books from the mid-1800's, along with more modern but exquisitely bound volumes. A dark wooden table and six carved wooden chairs were in the center of the room. A couch was placed against the wall and two ancient chairs guarded the door. Across the room, three stone steps led to another bedroom. This one less luxurious than the last but still steeped in age and an air of lost grandeur. Moving aside a heavy curtain I thought concealed a window, I was surprised to see a bricked-in doorway. Perhaps there were once additional rooms in this fantasy apartment.

Returning to the foyer, I entered the kitchen to the left. Surely, this was where meals fit for royalty were once prepared. There were 90 wine glasses neatly lined up like soldiers in the glass fronted cabinets. The 30 glass espresso cups each had a pewter holder with a delicate handle. The pots and pans were so large that my wife could actually sit in one for the comic picture we sent back to our friends in the States. A paella pan was easily three feet in diameter. Fortunately, there was also a shiny new set of human sized pans, an obvious recent purchase. The stove was a throwback to the 1940s with eight burners and a large oven below. A box of "strike anywhere" matches confirmed that there was no pilot light, and I would become adept at lighting the match and turning on the gas as if I had done this my entire life. The table in the center of the kitchen was eight feet long and four feet wide with a marble top. A wooden rolling pin had its home in a hole beneath the table, it too four feet long. I could imagine servants holding opposite sides of this cudgel as they rolled out massive sheets of dough for some delectable pasta or dessert.

The bathroom contained a full sized shower and a dark green pedestal sink. A modern toilet completed the room. On the walls photographs from Man Ray of women bathing and dressing adorned the walls. I could not discern if these were originals or copies. I did not dare to take them down for a closer look.

A knock on the door stopped our brief exploration. It was again the owner's son, this time with a welcome gift of six cream filled cannoli. We thanked him profusely, and he hastily departed with mountain goat like precision up the stairs.

Once the initial disorientation of this awe-inspiring apartment began to wear off. I walked through again, this time taking in details I clearly had missed both in the photographs on the web and in my first walk-through. A closer inspection of the frescoed ceiling would reveal deep and ominous looking stucco cracks, peeling paint, with faded and water stained portions of the once magnificent fresco. I could not help but wonder how long this crumbling glimpse of a bygone era could last. Certainly repairs would be expensive if even possible. There were portions of the fresco that seemed ready to fall into the living room with the right vibration. The couches turned out to be so worn that to sit meant to be just a few inches off the floor with wooden ribs of the massive furniture making deep indentations into my spine. Fortunately, the chairs did not suffer from this malady.

Stepping out onto the living room balcony left one perched directly above the canopy of the fish market. By early afternoon, the smell of not so fresh fish wafted through the doors with abandon. The odor was overwhelming. I would keep these doors closed most of our stay, but it would prove fruitless.

While standing on our balcony, I looked at the balcony to my left to see exposed wrought iron and crumbled concrete beneath it. The abandoned property next to us had clearly not been occupied for a long time. It looked as though it was a lasting relic of World War II. The war had not been kind to this city, and it was still recovering in some parts while other areas had been left to nature and time. I immediately stepped back into the apartment, wondering what the underside of our own balcony looked like. The next time we left the apartment, I made a mental note to look up and see if there was any danger of detachment.

Back in the kitchen, water pressure turned out to be a challenge. The faucet produced a slow stream of water that immediately backed up in the tiny drain. The drain would slowly empty itself if left alone. It proved sufficient for our limited cooking and cleaning. The window from the kitchen looked into a small shared courtyard that over the years became the holding cell for an amazing tangle of wires, pipes, trash, plastic pails, a few paint brushes and other detritus of the modern age. I surmised that no one considered this area as their own and as a consequence, no one took responsibility for it. From the window, there was a hanging clothes line structure with six plastic lines for outdoor drying. I understood immediately that if any article of clothing was to fall it would become a permanent addition to the courtyard decorations as there appeared to be no way to retrieve the fallen items. During our stay, I would avoid using this clothesline and dry our clothes inside hanging it from chairs and other available hangers. I could not help but notice that even the birds were not venturing into this miasma.

The balcony off of the master bedroom had a hanging planter with a half dead spiny plant struggling to stay alive. Previous visitors had obviously used this planter as an ashtray, failing to clean out the cigarette butts. It became my mission to revive this plant with a little pruning and daily doses of water. After the first watering and seeing the water immediately flow through the planter and pour onto the street below, I decided that watering time would be at night when there was less chance to drench passersby. I counted it as a small victory when I was rewarded with a singular flower two weeks later.

The first night was surreal. My wife had settled in with an air of royalty, her European upbringing seemingly having prepared her for this role. I allowed myself to be caught up in the moment and pretended to be someone grand, actually looking down on market shoppers and shopkeepers with a smile of tolerant magnanimity. We lay on the bed trying to appreciate that we were in an extraordinary place caught between ancient and modern times. The bedcover was a too heavy quilt with large too fluffy pillows. My wife retrieved a towel from the bathroom with which to fashion herself a pillow while I dutifully folded the quilt to the bottom of the bed. It was in this way we found sleep at last.

That night, I was awakened continually by the loud, low pitched hum of the electrical box echoing in the stairwell. It would click on seemingly every twenty minutes or so with a rattling hum. Just as I became accustomed to the noise it would click off leaving a deafening silence that would then be filled with the late night sounds of the street. A motorcycle roared down the narrow market street at 1:00 am. The sound bouncing wildly off of the ancient buildings. A loud, drunken argument between friends added to the charms of the night. The electrical box kept up its steady rhythm. I slept fitfully.

The next morning, I awakened to the sing-song bellowing of the vegetable seller directly across the street from our apartment. I would come to call him Giovanne-Melanzane after his sing-song call to shoppers and tourists alike and the fact that he had a dizzying amount of dark purple eggplant surrounding him. It helped that his name was actually Giovanni. The smell of fish was everywhere. The sun was shining brightly, and the ice under and over the fish was no match for the heat of the day, even at this early hour.

Ignoring the smells, I focused on my morning mission. I had seen a bakery next door, and I was determined to buy bread for our breakfast. As I stepped into the bathroom to splash some water on my face, I was greeted with an overwhelming smell of freshly baked bread. It felt like being in a cloud of yeasty, deliciously warm air. The vent from the bakery next door was positioned directly below the bathroom window. This was, without a doubt, the best smelling bathroom I had ever been in. But realistically, how long can one stay in the bathroom?

I dressed quickly, grabbed a handful of euros, and managed to navigate the stairs without falling. A switch next to the door turned on the lights over the stairs. I saw that the two motorcycles in the stairway were now gone. I wondered if one of them was the source of the symphony last night. Well, no matter.

Upon opening the door to the street, I was greeted by a few errant sardines who had escaped their boxes and lay just in front of the door, their dead eyes staring up at the sun. A small fishy river of milky colored ice water formed a pool in front of the raised threshold. I was able to deftly step over this hazard and noticed that as the fish boxes were emptied, they were stacked in a grand pile directly beneath our living room balcony. They would not be picked up until midnight by a loud, banging truck, and the very loud chatty workers that accompanied it. But I had a mission…fresh bread. I entered the bakery and was surprised to see no one in line. The store smelled wonderful. In halting Italian I asked for bread only to be told to come back in twenty minutes. It seemed I came in just as the last loaf was sold, and the next batch was baking. The only thing available was an odd looking rolled bread with a reddish sausage-looking piece of meat inside. Undeterred, I bought two, knowing full well that my wife would not eat mystery meat in the shape of a hot dog.

I headed back up the stairs. The light in the stairwell seemed to be timed to allow me to get to the fifteenth step before plunging me into darkness while I tried to see and climb the last ten steps. I would get used to this, and I would move faster over the next week. The sausage meat rolled in bread received the reception I had expected. I was proud to have made my first Sicilian purchase, a feat that seemed to be lost on my wife. I left the apartment amid a rolling of eyes and again descended the stairs, passed the friendly sardines, jumped the river of milky fish water and entered the bakery. This time I managed to buy a very fresh, warm baguette. As I gave the clerk a twenty euro note it was her turn to roll her eyes and gesture with her thumb rubbing her fingers. I understood there would not be change for this amount of euros. I checked my pocket for change coming up with a handful of coins of unknown value. I tried to ask the price, but she pointed to a small tray. I placed a bunch of the coins in the tray. She sorted through them taking about 20 cents and leaving the rest. I would get better at this as time progressed, and once I even got a smile of recognition. This was a bakery for locals, and I was certainly not one of them. By the week's end, I think I was grudgingly accepted as a recurring face in the early morning hours.

Returning to the apartment with actual bread made me an instant hero. We feasted on crusty, warm bread and were surprised when we finished the entire loaf. I went down and bought another.

CHAPTER III

The Grand Theaters of Palermo

Just down the street from Via Porto Carini is the amazing Teatro Massimo in Piazza Verde, straight out of the movie The Godfather III. It is a massive edifice some 83,000 square feet. In front, an iron fence separates the general public from the theater going public. Pass beyond the fence and you are entering a different world: grand, patrician, elegant. There are six Corinthian columns at the top of the stairs holding up the massive Greco-Roman entrance. Dramatic night lighting makes the theatre a true wonder to behold. I stood on the steps where Sofia Coppola stood when she was shot in the chest and then moved to the left wall of the stairs where the would-be assassin of Michael Corleone is murdered. It is impossible for me to not see those images as I looked at this monument to the past.

The structure is imposing and has an air of faded glory. It is an homage to the Greek, Roman and Norman architectural styles that one finds all over Palermo. It is the largest theater in Italy, and its facade is indeed grand with two massive lions on either side of the steep steps vigilantly watching the patrons as they arrive. The original construction took longer than expected, some thirty-three years of construction over-runs, politics and funding issues. It opened in 1897 and promptly closed after only two seasons. A grand re-opening in 1901 seemed to herald a new era. Then in 1974, as the mafia tightened its grasp on the city, Teatro Massimo closed for complete renovations. It would be 23 years before it would re-open in 1997. At that time, the city rebelled against mafia domination and found a new pride in its cultural icon. But now, just 20 years after the full restoration, the side doors are in desperate need of painting. The brown, wooden doors are full of peeling paint, and the iron fence is rusting. The old city of Palermo is to one side of the theater. On the other side a reminder of the mafia, blocks of concrete, uninspired housing that is in poor repair. There seems to be an air of resignation and acceptance that it will always be this way.

Teatro Massimo holds concerts both classical and modern in the gilded seven tiered interior. My wife and I sat in the fifth tier on the side. Our chairs free to be moved close to the vertiginous edge of the box. Looking to the right provided a view of the red curtained center box. This, of course, is where Michael Corleone sat during the performance in Godfather III. The gilding of every box on every tier is breathtaking. The entire theater is covered in old world red velvet and gilded baroque images of a bygone era. Returning my gaze to our box, I noticed the ceiling was cracked, a few small pieces were missing from the wood or stucco edges of the box. I instinctively moved my chair back a bit from the worn edge of the box. The air was warm and grew warmer throughout the performance. Jackets were removed, patrons fanned themselves with the programs. Attending the theater is not a mere cultural event. Families, obviously accustomed to seeing each other at these upper class events, hug, kiss, shake hands and clap each other on the back. The din of conversation echoing off the boxes is deafening. Only as the conductor enters does the floor become quiet and the conversations are stopped in favor of thunderous applause. The acoustics of the theater are legendary and our jazz concert will not be soon forgotten.

After the concert ended, there was a rush to the elevators, a slow walk through the lobby and then some loitering on the steps before descending into the piazza below. At night, Piazza Verde takes on a new significance. This is the meeting place of the youth of Palermo. Hundreds of young people sit along the sides of the theater, lounging against the iron fence. Dogs barked at passing patrons. Glass beer bottles rolled past as we walked toward the pedestrian street Via Maqueda with the crowd. I was surprised that no-one seemed to think this was unusual. Stepping over and around moving beer bottles was seemingly a practiced art, as was pretending that they did not exist. Songs were being sung and groups of young women eyed groups of young men who jumped and did handstands to impress them. Shirtless young men were breakdancing on cardboard to European hip hop played over ripped speakers with a raspy sound. I felt as though I was re-living a scene from 20 years ago. High heeled elegant women, men in suits, and the rough youth of yesterday were all occupying the Piazza Verde together.

Not far from this grand spectacle is another slightly less grand palace of the arts. Politeama Garibaldi Theater in Piazza Ruggero Settimo is the home of the Sicilian Symphony Orchestra. The late 1800's neoclassical building is crowned with a triumphal arch atop of which sits bronze statues depicting Apollo and Euterpe and two knights on horseback. It is an imposing group and a reminder of the days of the Italian Kings. Indeed, King Umberto I and Queen Margherita attended the opening of this theater in 1891. The building is an amphitheater-like round edifice with columns both at street level and on the second level providing support for the low domed roof, its pinkish-white walls reflecting the strong sunlight. An iron fence separates the theater from the piazza. It was meant as a complementary structure to Teatro Massimo to house less grand but perhaps more popular cultural events.

The Piazza itself is a stark and unforgiving stretch of concrete with little to no decoration except for a single statue of Ruggero Settimo in front of the theater. The summer sun is merciless as it bakes this unprotected arena. As I looked around, it was clear that some time ago, this was a grand square with impressive buildings on all sides. But as in most of Palermo, the buildings are now crumbling, the paint is peeling, and the grand brand names are housed in lifeless storefronts. There are ten rectangular concrete benches drenched in the sun across the top of the square near the street. A few brave souls were sitting here perhaps waiting for the bus. A group of students sat on the few steps in front of the statute in the middle of the square seemingly unfazed by the heat. There are a few low, round terra cotta planter boxes interspersed between the benches where wilted flowers struggle to survive the environment.

There was a children's competition on this day, and anxious parents and equally anxious children were massed in front of the theater. As I walked up to the iron gates, a young man in a white shirt and black tie stood in the opening blocking my entrance. My request, "Posso visitare?" was met simply with a polite but firm, "no, solo parenti." Undeterred, I circumnavigated the building to better view the architecture from each side. An impressive structure to be sure. In the weeks we were visiting, the theater remained closed but for this one day. While the grand Teatro Massimo steadily provided cultural fare, the Politeama would sadly provide only its exterior view.

CHAPTER IV
The Passeggiata

On Friday and Saturday nights, seemingly all of Palermo comes to the Via Maqueda for the evening passeggiata. This is much more than a simple walk down an ancient street. Barricades are placed by the local police so that this main street becomes a pedestrian only path leading all the way to the "Quatro Conti", a storied intersection with grand statues on each of the four corners dating from the 1600s. On both sides of Via Maqueda there are vendors selling everything from lightbulbs to fried Sicilian street foods. As we moved down the street at a leisurely pace, I noticed the stores went from Sicilian looking wares to Indian looking wares and finally to clothing stores with full length sequined outfits best suited to belly dancers.

The much ballyhooed street food of Palermo which every guide book mentioned was not in much evidence. A few stalls fronted the street offering a few Sicilian specialities such as arancine, delicious fried rice balls with a tiny bit of filling hidden in the center. Just a few blocks away, a store was offering twenty-five different types of this delicacy. There was everything from veal to chicken to vegetables to sweets. I stopped and bought two, melanzane and cheese. While others were content to simply sit on the benches that were on the street and eat these wondrous rice balls, I opted to take them back to the apartment for breakfast the next morning.

Before leaving on this Sicilian adventure, our Italian friends, a wonderfully expressive Sicilian couple, had provided us with a list of must-see attractions, among them: The Quatro Conti, the four corners. As our friend's wife began to explain the significance of the statutes found here, her husband, in a way only a true Sicilian could, looked at us, raised his shoulders and with his palms turned toward the sky said: "Ma, itsa just an interSECtion." Yes, but what an intersection! Piazza Vigilena is where Via Maqueda meets Via Corso Vittorio Emanuele and the early 1600's are in attendance. The statues from 1608 to 1620 on each separate corner depict in turn four Spanish kings, four seasons and four saints. There is a fountain on each corner, each wonderfully decorated. This was truly the most impressive intersection I had ever seen. The Spanish had left their grand baroque mark on this city as other rulers had left theirs. Throngs of tourists looked for the perfect place for a selfie or a group shot. I found the best pictures were taken from the middle of the intersection, a decidedly perilous place but from where you can hear the full colorful nature of the Sicilian language shouted from passing car windows.

The passeggiata continued as we retraced our steps back to the mobbed street in front of the Massimo Theater. To the right there are smaller alleyways from which come the most wonderful smells of Sicilian cuisine. Taking one of these led to a stone restaurant featuring Pesce Spada, the noble swordfish. I had an intense desire to get even with this fish, so we stopped and sat down on the interior of the restaurant. There were four tables on the extremely narrow street outside, but I did not relish the thought of eager tourists ogling my food as they passed. The interior was charming and rustic, the owner convivial. The swordfish was thinly sliced and well prepared with a tasty sauce on top. The caponata, a Sicilian eggplant dish, was also infused with swordfish. As I ate, I felt some sense of satisfaction that at least I would not be smelling this particular fish tonight in the apartment.

After dinner, we exited the small restaurant and turned left down the alleyway. We found ourselves in a large square with several restaurants, dozens of outdoor tables and hundreds of people. A procession was coming down the street. A statue of Christ on a large wooden crucifix with what looked like Christmas lights, all in blue and strung above his head, was being carried on a bier by a dozen men dressed in red and gold. They had to make a turn down a narrow alleyway which became a comical exercise. Back and forth they went, advancing only a few feet each time with decidedly unchristian cursing as they bumped, scraped and banged against walls, restaurant tables and patrons. Finally, the turn completed, the priest began a prayer as he walked in front of the crucifix, and all present solemnly intoned the words. The procession faded down the street towards a cathedral.

Returning to Piazza Verde, we were greeted by groups of men wearing large feathered hats and uniforms all carrying various small brass instruments. Some of the hats looked as though entire great black roosters had been impressed into duty to sit atop the heads of these proud soldiers. They stood in circles, and music blared from their collective efforts. Some sang, some played and all were well oiled. The music was mostly off key, the singing mostly shouted words, but the sense of camaraderie was clearly evident. These were all brothers in some military order in friendly competition. I asked several people what was happening, but a tourist was not expected to understand and explanations were short. A military observance was the best I could learn. The music, singing and pageantry lasted far into the night, and we were happy to witness this extraordinary spectacle even if we did not understand the significance. We marched our way home leaving the music behind us.

Via Porto Carini was quiet with few people walking the street. A few dogs laid in the middle of the street, but none were menacing. As we approached the apartment, the smell of fish and a pile of empty fish boxes rose to greet us. Aah, home at last.

CHAPTER V
Good Continuation

About half way down Via Maqueda as I walked towards the famous intersection of Quattro Conti, on the right-hand side of the street I found the most wonderfully intimate corner wine bar. It serves only Sicilian wines. The sign written in chalk on the exterior says, in English, "Wine 5 euros." I peered inside to find a very narrow shop, four tables along the left wall where four could sit at each table, that is, if you were really comfortable with each other. Otherwise, two people would fit nicely, and the other chairs could hold bags or coats. On the right wall was a bar for standing while drinking, and in the back a larger table and another to its left. The improbable sound of classic American Jazz floated through the air. Billy Holiday was singing the blues, and I was transported back to a time of speakeasies and forbidden pleasures. There was no one inside, but perhaps that was due to the time of day. It was only 3:00 in the afternoon and the street was rather empty of tourists. My wife and I went inside and sat at the third table on the left. This was far enough in to be enveloped by the atmosphere of the place and close enough to the door to still watch the passing street activity.

It wasn't long before a young woman came from the back speaking to us in Italian and saying what I imagined was "Sorry, I did not hear you come in." She quickly understood that we were not well versed in Italian and the conversation turned to English at which she was quite proficient. We learned that the Sicilian wines in this bar were carefully chosen from many available. I did not say that I had so far been unimpressed with the selection of wines from Sicily and listened to this woman who seemed to know about vines, winery processes and terroir. I had heard of and tasted the Donnafugatta labeled wines and sampled the Sicilian primitivo grapes which are claimed to be the precursor of a modern Zinfindel. What I saw now was that this young woman possessed a passion not often seen and a wealth of knowledge about her country's wines. We were soon presented with a champagne style wine called Murgo. It was light, complex in its bouquet and wonderfully full of citrus and peaches. What was even more wonderful was the thoughtful look and knitted brow of the young woman serving us who both smelled and tasted the wine before pouring us a generous glass each.

I asked about her life, her family and her work. She was kind enough to tell us about her husband, an olive oil worker now idled by the seasonal nature of the work and her mother who lived in another village but whom she saw often. She became passionate when admitting that it was her desire to have a wine bar of her own. She had traveled with her boss to learn about the trade, the wines and the various producers in Sicily. She spoke with a faraway look in her eyes almost as if acknowledging that this dream may never come to fruition. She confided that she and her husband did not have the means to start such an endeavor, and it seemed unlikely that they would be able to accumulate that much without outside help which was not likely forthcoming. Her attention turned again to the wines. She selected another Sicilian gem and repeated the explanation of provenance and terroir, tasting and pouring. Her choice was impeccable and we again savored the nectar of the Sicilian gods. I asked about getting something to eat and learned that no food could be served since they were not a restaurant. However, they were able to serve cold hors d'oeuvres. Olives with caponata appeared a short time later and we enjoyed this simple feast of flavors with our wine.

As we chatted with our hostess about life in these United States and the differences between our country and hers, two men entered the shop with an air of arrogant authority. From my limited Italian language ability, it seemed that these were wine producers who were somewhat insistent that their products be featured at this establishment. Our thoughtful hostess sounded very sincere and apologetic as she explained that she was a mere worker and such decisions were made by her boss who was presently not available. As the two men left, I could not help but recall how business in Palermo was tainted by the ever-present mafia and wondered if this was a request or a demand on this small business.

Later, the owner appeared, and proved to be a wonderful throwback to more chivalrous times. He was sporting a multi-colored scarf, a pullover sweater and a huge smile. As soon as he entered, he took my wife's hand and kissed it, complementing her in Italian. He was the absolute image of the older gentleman who still believed he held sway with the ladies. His pleasant affect was contagious. Later, he would be seen chatting up a small group of Swedish young women who were enjoying the unlikely find of a jazz bar in Palermo. He had a twinkle in his eye that would not be extinguished.

Our hostess kept us informed regarding the wines and re-filled our glasses as we requested. I never asked for and never saw the five-euro wine listed on the sign out front. Our wines were eight and ten euros a glass, still a great bargain for the stunning wines we tasted. Conversation was always pleasant, and we formed an easy bond with our hostess during the few short weeks we would be exploring her city. We returned to this wine bar several more times, usually in the evening when patrons spilled onto the street in animated conversation. Each time we were given a warm welcome. Each time our hostess turned to leave us she would smile sweetly and say, "Good Continuation!" At first we looked at each other with puzzlement and tried to figure out what she meant, but in time we could only think that this was indeed a "good continuation."

CHAPTER Vi

The Fortress

Our guidebook, the internet and our map all clearly depicted a fortress near the port. Walking in that direction we passed several areas one could only call distressed. The center of Palermo is a cluster of crumbling buildings on street after street, all bristling with satellite dishes. The passage of time, World War II and the mafia are all to blame for the current state of the city. Rather than repair the old building to their former grandeur, blocks of rectangular apartments were built outside the center. The mafia, and its control of construction contracts and materials, is largely responsible for the current look of the city. Both politicians and "godfathers" had become rich with construction overruns, ghost jobs and outright bribes. Now, the hastily and cheaply built apartment blocks show a premature aging process: concrete is cracked, balconies are detaching from the main structures, walls are crumbling and no one seems to be interested in repairs to most of these eyesores. To be sure, there is the occasional remodel. The apartment next to our rental was being renovated, or should I say gutted, to be replaced by luxury apartments you could buy for a mere half million euros. I hoped the new owners would like the smell of fish.

While traversing these side streets on our way to the fortress, we saw much laundry being dried outside windows on lines strung across streets and sometimes between apartments. It created a colorful picture on even the most rundown of side streets. Rounding a corner, we came upon one of the largest urban garbage piles I had ever seen-easily twenty feet tall, it contained rubbish, mattresses, rags, car parts and several cats. I wondered if the residents has refused to pay the "pizzu," a bribe to keep the garbage pick-up current. The mafia still shakes down shopkeepers, apartment owners and any business in the city. The result is a stunning lack of progress and an attitude of resignation among the people. Recently, there is a brave "anti-pizzu' movement among some shopkeepers who proudly display signs indicating they will not pay any bribes to anyone. This is not an easy stance to take and some businesses have mysteriously caught fire in the middle of the night. Hopefully, the movement catches on and the mafia becomes less of a threat to the proud Sicilians trying to prosper in this environment.

As it turns out, the fortress we were looking for is a low pile of ancient stones with no access for visitations. We walked past the site without realizing that it was there. We ended up at the port. Expensive yachts, fishing boats and a very nice concrete quay made for a pleasant afternoon. We found one seaside restaurant that seemed serviceable, but as it was bathed in the hot Sicilian sun, we passed the opportunity to dine.

Retracing our steps for the third time, I finally saw the excavated wall poking its head above the level of an immense field overgrown with dry weeds. There was a fence surrounding the fortress with an ominous sign indicating that trespassers were not allowed. We watched as an obviously homeless man hopped the fence and relieved himself on an ancient fortress wall. He then walked around the wall and down some steps, disappearing into the trash strewn excavation. Perhaps it was best to do as the signs said and not trespass beyond the fence. Clearly, there was no money in restoration of the fortress, and it sits alone in an abandoned field with no one in attendance save the forgotten few who sleep here at night.

CHAPTER VII
Norman Grandeur

At Quattro Conti, if you turn your back to the sea and begin walking you will pass several churches, hotels and innumerable shops. On the right just as the street comes to an end is the truly magnificent Palazzo dei Normanni. This is easily the best preserved building in Palermo. The structure is imposing and breathtaking in its grandeur. It is a UNESCO World Heritage Site and with good reason. Palazzo Reale, as it is known locally, was begun by the Arabs in the ninth century and built on top of the ruins of a Roman church that was built, in turn, on top of a Punic fortresses. The classic Arabian style architecture is still visible in several areas although Greek and Roman influences are everywhere. Ruggero II conquered Sicily in 1072 and made the palace the seat of government. Palermo became the capital of the Kingdom of Sicily, and the palace was extended and rebuilt in areas with magnificent gardens in enclosed courtyards. Aside from admiring the exterior of the building, which itself will leave the viewer in awe, the most visited and gilded addition is the Cappella Palatina, a wondrous private chapel built by Ruggero II from 1132 to about 1143. As you enter the chapel, the soft glow of golden mosaics overtake your senses. Every wall, every corner, every crevice is inlaid with golden and painted tiles depicting scenes of nature, saints and personages from Christianity's best biblical stories. These are some of the best preserved Byzantine mosaics in the world. There are flowers, animal life, a dozen saints, and a golden alter wall that will take your breath away. Adam and Eve are caught in the act of eating the forbidden fruit. The figure of Christ Pantocrator, unsmiling and slightly severe, looks out from the apse and cupola, in his left hand a book while his right hand blesses the faithful. The ceiling is a wooden honeycomb structure depicting animal hunts and scenes of nature.

It is nearly impossible to take in all this beauty in a single visit. While trying to see and photograph the interior there were constant and incessant groups of tourists of differing languages shuffling in large groups with their fearless and informed leaders often contradicting themselves with differing dates, differing untrue anecdotes and stopping to point out the obvious. The chapel is best viewed in solitary reflection. Only then will the visitor feel the power of the artistic endeavor and perhaps gain some personal insight. The royal throne and final resting place of Ruggero II are here for viewing. It is a solemn and reverent experience to slowly walk this chapel, admire its great beauty and contemplate your place in the universe.

It is difficult to understand how this magnificent palace was abandoned and fell into ruin. Only thanks to the Spanish Viceroys in 1555 was it re-discovered, resurrected as a royal residence and restored to its former grandeur. The current care-takers have made the palace the seat of the semiautonomous regional government of Sicily. As such, many areas are off limits to ordinary mortals. Still, standing in front of such a wonderful and ancient structure cannot help but fill one's head with visions of civilizations past.

To the right of this palace is a small street that winds its way back to the market in Via Porto Carini. As the road begins, and visible beneath glass structures, are the foundations of the palace. The street is narrow and dark and unevenly cobble-stoned. Walking here after dark is an adventure. Soon one arrives at a small piazza. The guide books tell me this is a famous piazza, but all I can see is a small kiosk selling panninis and soft drinks and a lot full of parked cars. Several locals were gathered here sampling the wares and discussing the events of the day. This is not a place for outsiders and we continued our walk until the distinct odor of fish told us we were home.

CHAPTER VIII

The Walk to Bagheria

Take any street to the water and turn right. The port is full of boats of all sizes for fishing, sailing and heavy working. Passing this will lead to a waterfront park. The park has a concrete walkway near the sea. The park itself is sparse with vegetation. From a distance it appears greenish in color but fades to a brownish green the closer one gets. There are few trash receptacles in sight and the happy residents of Palermo have left their mark and their residue behind. Sticking to the concrete path yields a beautiful sea view and a glimpse of a long coastline.

I had decided to walk on the coast as far as my feet could go, calculating how long it would take to return before dark. While I do not recommend this to anyone, it did yield some fascinating sights. For instance, on one stretch of beach, unfortunately soiled with trash, we were followed for some distance by a young man leading a horse. He suddenly stripped off his shirt and led the horse into the water. In seconds they were some 20 yards from shore, both swimming in circles. The man holding on the rope around the horse's head, and the horse following the man as he swam in slow circles. My wife and I watched and marveled at this unusual sight wondering at the strange bond these two must have.

As we continued our walk the rubble of the city's outskirts was everywhere to behold. Nearly every building is cracked and peeling, paint faded and streets in need of resurfacing. Once again, the mafia controlled construction industry that built these eyesores skimped on concrete and used inferior materials. The result is an ugly reminder that the honorable men of the mafia are nothing more than pretenders, petty thieves preying on their Sicilian brethren. Trash is liberally strewn about, and one can almost feel the hopeless resignation among the inhabitants. Still, there is an exuberance of life in the children and the noisy family gatherings. Men can be observed sitting at tables in a faded cafe drinking espresso and discussing politics, soccer and women. There is an unspoken division here between the sexes. Men sit with men, women with women and younger people with each other. A man who sits with the women is viewed by the other men as something less than a man, or worse, as a threat to their women. Social culture remains somewhat primitive and rough. I perceived that this would be a difficult place to grow up. The young boys are tough and learn to bully at an early age, but perhaps this prepares them for the inevitable hardships that Sicilian life will bring.

As the sun reached the late afternoon, we decided to turn around and walk back. We took a slightly different route but were greeted with the same drab scenery. Cars whizzed past on the main thoroughfare, horns honking and voices raised. People were everywhere hurrying to get home. A wrong turn took us down an abandoned road with a very high, faded brick and concrete wall on one side, and what looked like an abandoned industrial factory on the other. This rusted reminder of an industrial past was nestled in a large field, where the weeds were competing for what sparse moisture came their way. Mercifully, we reached the sea, and keeping the water to our right, we found our way back to the port. The sun was just setting and its reflection on the sea along with the long shadows cast by the many masts of the moored sailboats shimmering on the surface transformed this into a magical view. One could almost forget the grit of the day and lose oneself in the brilliance of the Sicilian Sea.

CHAPTER IX

The Road to Monreale

In Piazza Verde there is a taxi stand. Usually there are two or three taxis waiting to take the tourists to various destinations. The honesty of the drivers varies considerably. The guidebooks all suggest that 20 euros will get you to Monreale some eight kilometers up the mountainside on an easy road. I was quoted 40 euros. Of course, the meter in the taxi did not work. The driver in the next taxi just smiled broadly and indicated that I could not change to his taxi since he was second in line. Fleecing of tourists was a game, and I had just lost. We got into the taxi, and he turned left onto Via Maqueda and then onto Via Roma driving in the opposite direction from our destination. The taxi driver said nothing, but I had the impression that he wanted to make the ride longer to justify the cost. Eventually we began climbing the mountain but inexplicably took a turn down a very narrow street that was blocked by a large truck. Our driver cursed and turned into a private driveway and stopped. Here we waited for several minutes while the truck maneuvered and finally cleared the road. The taxi turned around, headed back down the mountain until he joined the large and easy road to

Monreale. Turning up the mountain it was just a few minutes drive to the church we had come to see.

The exterior of the cathedral is surprisingly angular and lacks ornamentation when compared to the many smaller churches in Palermo. The courtyard to the side of the Cathedral is a bounded by landscaping, hedges and benches facing a fountain and statuary in the center. The statue is that of a young man in the center of the fountain who appears to be standing atop a giant two headed sea monster which he has captured from the depths. His face is set in a grimace of strength as he hauls the beast up with a knotted rope. Alas, the power and majesty of this scene is somewhat lessened by the pigeon resting on his sinewy arm and another sitting quietly on his head, both seemingly oblivious to the danger the sea monster represents.

Walking down the street along the side of the cathedral allows one to see the intricate designs and Moorish influences of the church. Multiple intersecting arches, rosette mosaics and rounded towers dominate the view. The tile work on the upper stories reveals delicate and beautiful patterns. There are embedded columns accenting the arches towering some fifty feet overhead. The angular plain look of the main entrance is nowhere to be found here. This magnificent exterior is not much seen by the passing crowds, most whom head directly for the main door with a guide hurrying them along. A perimeter walk reveals a truly exceptional architectural wonder.

Across from the largely unseen side of the cathedral is a small perfectly picturesque neighborhood. It is a warren of small cobblestone streets beautifully manicured with potted plants, arched doorways and ivy covered balconies. As we marvel at this seemingly idyllic community, a lone figure is noted on a balcony above looking directly at us. The two paws stretched out over the balcony edge and a low growl help us to understand that we should probably keep to the tourist track and not loiter in front of these homes. We left just as the barking commenced.

The unforgiving sun is strong and bright. Touristic trinkets, drinks, bright handbags, painted plates and postcards are for sale from a cart next to the fountain. The street unfortunately has no quaint architecture to its many buildings. Just past the Cathedral and up a few steps there is another small street with a few touristic restaurants. A brightly painted Sicilian donkey cart, complete with a stuffed caricature of a donkey wearing a straw hat festooned with flowers, greets us tourists. Trattoria Monreale and Pizzeria Monreale offered some refuge from the sun with two giant white shade umbrellas. The cane backed chairs, red checkerboard tablecloths and wood fired oven pizza menu was obviously designed for the day tripper with little time for a

The entrance doors to the cathedral are a marvel to see. The bronze doors are truly magnificent and reminiscent of the baptistry doors in Florence. The biblical scenes are in beautiful bas relief and I passed my hand over the hand craved scenes soaking in the feel of the 12th century that produced them, only then noticing the sign that indicated we were all being watched by a camera somewhere in this entryway. I removed my hand but not before caressing the dragon being slain by Saint George.

The interior of the cathedral of Monreale is as impressive as the Capella Palatina. It also has a gilded interior that takes your breath away. Christ the Pantocreator is here as well, with a benevolent look and holding God's laws. The wooden ceiling is painted and we were told that it was damaged in a fire so we were looking at the replacement from the early 1800s.

On the trip back, the cost was 15 euros. Our driver cursed at his fellow countryman for cheating us and explained that some thought to steal was permitted if the victim was a well heeled tourist. He felt this was giving his city a bad reputation and was quite passionate in his denunciation of such a system. While in this impassioned state he looked to his right at a field that was trash strewn and unkempt and gestured with his hand. "Look at this! Can you believe it!" He then launched into a most interesting tale. "You know," he said, "this is the fault of the Arabs." But no, not the Arabs living in Palermo now, but the

Arabs who came in the 900s and left their mark on the city's architecture. According to our driver, who had obviously studied
this fascinating history, the Arabs of that time threw all their
trash and garbage into the streets. That was how this bad habit
started and it continues to this day. He assured us that true Sicilians would never behave like this. He confirmed this with a
shake of his head and a disgusted look. He returned us to Piazza
Verde and from there we followed the smell of fish back to our
apartment.

CHAPTER X
CEFALU

After two weeks of living with the unrelenting and over-whelming smell of fish, I decided that we needed a break from this odious ambiance. Looking at a map revealed that we were very close to Cefalu, a small seaside town that promised a picturesque and interesting diversion. Speaking with the owner of our apartment, he assured us that Cefalu was a vacation destination that all Sicilians considered to be the perfect summer getaway. He would lock up our apartment during the time we would be gone. As we had rented the Palermo apartment for a month, we were able to leave some of the luggage behind and concentrated on where to stay in Cefalu. I settled on a small resort that had twenty thatched roof casitas terraced into the hillside such that all had a magical view of the sea. Its name, Calinica, sounded more Greek than Italian, but the Greeks had left their mark on this island long ago and many places had old Greek names.

Getting out of Palermo by car is an adventure not for the faint-hearted. I have learned that in Sicily, lane markings and signal lights are mere suggestions, seemingly not mandatory. If the road can accommodate more cars than the lanes suggest, then by all means, add more cars. As I pulled up to the red-light, cars were stopped in the three marked traffic lanes and in two imaginary traffic lanes. Once across the intersection, five cars would be vying for space in the two lanes that continued forward on the opposite side. The cars in the imaginary lanes were within inches of scraping the cars in the actual lanes. Apparently, I have an exaggerated sense of necessary space, as no one else seemed concerned about this claustrophobic cluster. There was nothing to do but hug the bumper of the car in front and hope for the best. With much braking, hand gestures and loud unintelligible curses, the five lanes became two lanes and all was well. In this way it took just over an hour to get through the city.

I had long given up relying on street signage. There was no chance to even read a sign when concentrating on not playing bumper cars in the middle of Palermo. By keeping the sun to my left, I followed various larger roads until I was mercifully moving far from the madding crowd and into a place of relative serenity.

A winding coastal road crossed and re-crossed a railroad track. Finally, a sign no larger than my license plate announced that Calinica was near. Following a narrow road to the very end, past a shuttered resort on the right, led to the wonderland that is Calinica. A gravel parking lot baking in the sun and a small office building were the only indications that we had arrived. The office was small and unimpressive, and I wondered if I had made a mistake believing the internet explanation of this resort. We were met by Matteo, the affable and capable manager who rode up on his motorcycle. He took our bags, somehow balanced them on the motorcycle and sped off toward our casita. Before leaving, he assured us that paradise was just around the corner and slightly downhill.

A winding concrete walkway led from the reception to each of the units. The landscape was typical Mediterranean- somewhat dry and rocky with a few robust trees and bushes along the paths. Mateo did not lie. Just around the path and down a small hill, the view that struck us squarely in the eyes was truly stunning. An impossibly blue sea glinted and swayed below. The rocky coast was accented with greenery proudly jutting beyond rock ledges. The sea gently buffeted the shore. There were no cars to be seen. There were no crowds of tourists jostling for the best selfie position. At the water's edge, a wooden deck was a backdrop to a pebble beach with reed mats reaching into the water, the better to protect out touristic feet.

We walked leisurely to unit twenty-eight, and arrived to find the bags neatly lined up at the door. The room was a circular hut with a thatched palapa style roof. The interior was divided by a half wall. On one side of the wall we found a queen-

every space between the sea and the mountain was cluttered with buildings and one was treated to a view of rooftops and angular shapes that blended into a marvelous mirage. The rise of the 12th century Norman Cathedral over the town gave it a mythical appearance. The dense development stopped at the foot of the mountain which was a vertically imposing wall of rock over just 1200 feet above sea level called La Rocca di Cefalu. In ancient times the summit hosted, in turn, a Greek temple, a Roman fortress, an Arab citadel and finally a Norman castle. Sadly, the ruins of these past glories are somewhat limited. The Salita Saracena is the somewhat narrow stone staircase that winds up La Rocca and leads to the summit. It is uneven and not well tended, but does provide a moderate workout for the thirty minutes of stair climbing effort. The archeological park begins at the top, and one can still see the outlines of the Temple of Diana said to have been built in the perhaps the fourth or fifth century BC on top of an earlier ninth century BC site. This later became a Byzantine church. One can also see the crenelated walls of the former castle. A large modern metallic cross, affectionately known as the La Rocca Cross, and visible at night from all of Cefalu, resembles a giant scaffolding adorned with electric lights. It has been erected in the ruins of the ancient courtyard of the temple overlooking the town. It was perhaps not the best idea and looks out of place and time, but each suc-

sea was truly a sight to behold. All this made the cold, crisp white wines from Mount Etna taste all the more exceptional.

If one were to walk Cefalu without stopping to admire, purchase and eat, it would take a mere two hours to walk through the entire town. The highlight of course, is the Norman Cathedral with its twin towers jutting high above the surrounding landscape of low-slung buildings. The reddish brick color of the Cathedral sets it apart from the more white washed look of the surrounding town. More than a dozen stone steps lead to a gated courtyard anchored by four statues sitting on large rectangular columns serving as pillars for the wrought iron fence separating the town from the sacred ground of the cathedral. Beyond the fence, the facade of the building presents an impressive and imposing look. The two towers on either side of the main doors are rectangular and stand four stories high. Each has somewhat Moorish style windows, arches set within further arched niches. The lower windows are singular giving way to two double windows and finally ending in a single upper window on one tower and a double window on the opposite side. These final windows are housed in a smaller, but nonetheless impressive, crenelated bell towers. The final reaches of each tower are triangular sections that point to the heavens. Between the towers on the ground level there are three enormous arches leading to the cathedral doors. These are topped by another row of intersecting arches and finished with a third and final upper row of twelve single arches. From the courtyard, the towers and facade create a sense of awe that one feels the closer one gets. The overall feeling is a more insignificant sense of self and a greater sense that something much more significant is lying just beyond the doors.

The interior does not disappoint. Here, as in Monreale and Palermo, the Norman Cathedral alter wall is adorned with 12th century gold mosaics. No wonder that it was included as a World Heritage site by UNESCO. On this wall one again finds a mosaic of Christ the Pancreator looking down, unsmiling, holding a book in one hand and possibly providing a blessing with the other. There are saints, apostles and angels lining the lower reaches of the altar wall. The ceiling is a wooden V shaped construction with heavy beams stretched across the arched stone walls leading to the altar. Large columns line either side of the church with the upper walls and side walls devoid of ornamentation which focuses one's attention toward the beautiful altar wall. There are no tourist crowds here, and one gets the sense that this is a true place of worship for the believing locals who inhabit this picturesque village.

Walking toward the center of the town one finds Lavatorio Medievale on Via Vittorio Emanuele. This could be easily overlooked save for the sound of splashing water, which upon investigation brings one to a nearly hidden, obviously ancient, Arab built public washhouse. There is a single small stone plaque dated 1665 indicating its existence. The plaque is old, but the wash house is much, much older. Several stone steps lead to cavernous opening with several basins and walkways between them. There are a number of what look to be stone reservoirs fed by an underground stream, the River Cefalino, all channeling water through twenty-two cast iron openings into a large stone basin lined with stone benches. Many of the cast iron spouts are fashioned as lion's heads spitting water into the waiting pool. One can imagine Arab women washing their clothes in this grand basin and gossiping about their neighbors. I was told that the original wash house was destroyed and this one built in the early 1500s. Legend has it that the tears of a young woman who accidentally caused the death of her lover is the original source of the water. Of course, I now had to taste the water pouring from a nearby lion's mouth and found it not the salty tears of a beauty, but the pure, cold, fresh water of a mountain stream. On this day, only a few tourists were dangling their feet into the surprisingly icy pool of water. Arched tunnels bring the water to the sea as they have for hundreds of years.

At night, the lights from the restaurants and hotels reflect off of the sea creating a mystical canvas of shimmering illusion. As the sun sets, a golden light trail surrounded by colors of deep red and violet leads from the setting sun to the shore and then as the sun sinks below the horizon, the lights from the village begin their reflective dance of elongated shapes and ephemeral visions. This is a magical time of the evening, and the shore is populated by lovers. An immense sense of calm, the only sound being the gentle lap of the sea against the sand, infects one with the feeling that in the end, all will be well.

The beaches in summer are depicted in postcards as being a sea of multicolored umbrellas with several hundred Italians all standing in the water near the shore. On the days we were there, umbrellas were few and people were not yet venturing into the cooler waters of the spring season. To be sure, children, who are immune to such considerations as cold water, were happily splashing about as their parents watched from a short distance. Animated conversation could be heard, and groups of young girls eyed groups of young boys who performed acrobatic feats on the sand hoping to prove their masculinity and be noticed.

Later, back at Calinica, I ventured into the water to combat the heat of the late afternoon. A woven mat was thoughtfully set out on top of the beach rocks making the trek to the water an easy walk. Once at the shore's edge, the unevenness of the rocky shore made actually entering the water a challenge. After two halting giant steps, I plunged in, keeping my surf walkers on. The water was refreshing and bracingly cold. I swam to a very large nearby rock jutting high out of the Mediterranean like a small island. In my mind's eye, I climbed this rock and proudly stood atop its summit proclaiming it as my domain and defying anyone to take it from me. The photographs taken by my wife show a small figure treading water at the base of a towering rock structure with no hope of getting close enough to touch, let alone climb, the steep and slippery slope. The figure is alternately waving both arms above his head as if fighting off some invisible predatory seabirds or floating serenely with only head and feet visible from the shore. My wife has told me that at times I looked like an otter, basking in the shallows. To this day, I swear it's not me.

CHAPTER XI

On the Road to Taormina

Driving in most Italian cities, and Palermo in particular, can be challenging. Drivers yell and curse from their windows, hands and arms wildly gesticulating. Each driver is convinced of his own prowess behind the wheel. Apparently, all male Italian drivers are descended from the famous race car driver, Mario Andretti. Who was I to argue. As a result, all the commotion is roundly ignored as it cannot possibly be directed at any particular individual, each perfect in his own right. That is, of course, unless you are a tourist. In that case, you are always wrong and obviously stupid, and each gesture is clearly directed at you personally, or so it seems.

I followed a sign with a large arrow that read "TUTTI DIREZIONI." How could you go wrong? A road that leads everywhere. Very convenient and, as it turned out, very true. This road led to the main highway from whence you could indeed go every direction.

I followed as close behind another car as I dared while listening to my newly purchased GPS tell me to take the third exit on the roundabout. My GPS has a vaguely British accent and uses terms like "roundabout" rather than the apparently pedestrian "traffic circle." There was a small incoming street to my right that apparently did not count as an exit, and I found myself leaving the roundabout on the second exit while my GPS dutifully said: "Recalculating." I imagined that I heard it say: "What part of third exit did you not understand?" While it was recalculating, I made a quick and thoroughly illegal u-turn and tried to re-enter the roundabout, knowing that if I did not do this, I would be making several hopeless right turns possibly miles away until directed back to this spot.

There are rules to driving in a traffic circle. If necessary, the entering car stops at the line before entering waiting for that fleeting and elusive break in traffic that will allow a seamless entry into the traffic circle. There are usually two but sometimes three circular lanes to choose from. There are often five to six exits to choose from. The farther your exit, the deeper into the circle you drive. You then carefully merge through the lanes to exit your chosen path. The exits are all marked with signs announcing where that particular exit leads. If you miss the exit due to traffic, you simply go around again until your exit magically appears again in front of you.

Apparently there is another thoroughly Italian way to navigate a traffic circle. This involves stepping on the gas and quickly entering the roundabout oblivious to other traffic, swerving around large trucks and entering the left most lane in the circle. Then as your exit approaches you curse and wave one hand out of the window in a meaningful gesture to the cars around you. A raised middle finger I would understand, but a raised fist with the thumb stuck between the index finger and the middle finger is lost on me. Then, as your exit becomes imminent, you aim the car at a forty-five degree angle toward the exit, blast the horn, curse and wave again at the other cars who are now swerving to avoid you. After successfully exiting, you shake your head at the unbelievable stupidity of the other drivers on the road who should never have been there in the first place.

Naturally, I followed the Italian driver in front of me hugging his bumper and imitating his movements. I found myself in the third lane of the circle when the car I was dutifully following suddenly drove toward his exit at a rather steep angle. I continued around and tried to read the signs stating our destination while the GPS tried to catch up. Each sign unfortunately announced at least five destinations, a highway, a town, a city and a landmark or two. By the time I read two of the possible destinations, I had passed the exit and was on to attempting to read the next signpost. In this way I became intimately familiar with this particular traffic circle, driving around it five times until my GPS mercifully told me to "Take the next exit." In order to do so and not complete yet another revolution, I aimed my car at the exit, blasted my horn, waved my arm out the window and hoped for the best. A moment later I was happily moving toward my next traffic circle with the confidence of an Italian race car driver.

This traffic circle system of driving would serve me well until the day a hesitant older Italian woman in what appeared to be an even older Fiat, her gray hair in a kerchief, decided to stop in the left lane of the traffic circle to look to her right to see if any other car was coming into the roundabout. This, of course, as I was looking to my right trying to read the destination sign on the exit. The ensuing collision was light but nevertheless shocking for both of us. I gestured for her to move out of the circle and stop on the side of the road. We both got out to inspect the damage. As I was asking in broken Italian why she stopped, she was asking in gesticulating Italian why I hit her. My Italian was poor and all I could manage was to tell her the damage wasn't very bad: "non ce malo." I understood that she was telling me to look where I was going next time. In fact, the only damage was a line of dirt where my bumper had struck hers. I wiped her bumper clean and she saw there was nothing more. I reentered my car and drove off feeling bad that she seemed confused at what to do next and remained standing at her car as I left. I still wonder if I was supposed to do anything else but there seemed to be no harm. After this experience, I

Petrusa bridge, that took three cars with it as it too collapsed near Agrigento a year prior to this more recent tragedy.

I chose to drive the old and more interesting coastal road rather than drive through the mountains crossing the desert dry hilltops of central Sicily. This is a much longer but infinitely more satisfying drive. I admit this decision was contributed to by my own vanity at wanting to see Santo Stefano Di Camastra, one of many towns that bear my name. I had heard that this town was known for its pottery and was determined to stop and have a look. As one drives east from Palermo along the coast, roughly following the railroad tracks, there are many small towns that are announced by the vibrant colors of the pottery shops lining the main road through the town. Each town seems to have its identifying color scheme differentiating it from all the others. As one moves east, the colors go from bright yellows to blood orange. The most striking of the colors are found in Santo Stefano Di Camestra. The pottery there has such a deep orange color that it appears as if the sun is setting in each plate and ceramic vessel. My first glimpse of this pottery came from plates and pots oddly set out against the hillside on the right side of the road at a curve. Around the curve, several pottery shops lined the road on the left proudly displaying the blood orange colors and intricate patterns that have made this town a center for ceramics. Since the 1500s, the making of bricks, tiles and pottery has been the mainstay of this town. An unfortunate land-slide in 1682 caused the town to be relocated and given a new name. Santo Stefano Di Mistretta, now destroyed, became Santo Stefano Di Camastra, honoring the Duke of Camastra, the hu-manitarian and enlightened aristocrat who planned the recon-struction after the landslide.

The colors in Santo Stefano are indeed striking and sim-ply cannot be ignored by the passing drivers. Geometric shapes in the style of Louis the Fourteenth are truly beautiful to behold. The sun glints off of the highly polished ceramics and pulls one into the shops for a closer look. At this point there were five separate shops all selling similar wares, each more beautiful than the last. A leisurely stroll through the shops was easily overwhelming as thousands of ceramic pieces all vied for atten-tion. Alas, the sun was actually setting, the sky taking on the blood orange of the surrounding ceramics and Taormina beck-oned in the distance.

CHAPTER XII

The Commune of Taormina

Our hotel was located on the beach at the edge of town. Following the signs to the center of the beach road left one with two options, turn right or turn left. Fortunately, there was a sign listing all the hotels in the area and arrows pointing variously right or left. We went to the right after locating the name of our hotel, and it was an easy drive to the edge of town. The entrance of the hotel was up a small hill from the beach and encircled with bougainvillea, nearly hiding the entrance. The hotel was actually built into the hillside such that you entered from the fourth floor and proceeded down to the first floor and out to the beach. The reception desk was manned by a single silver-haired man who looked over his reading glasses at these two late season arrivals. I told him in Italian that we had a reservation for six nights, gave my name and waited while he searched the papers on the desk. Our existence now validated by a deeply buried fax, he smiled broadly and presented the keys to our room. I was sure this was a prepaid reservation and he was just as sure it was not. Rather than argue, I presented a credit card and made a mental note to call the service I had used to sort this out later. Best not to argue in a language you haven't mastered.

This decision proved to be the right one as I later determined that I had not prepaid this hotel but rather had only reserved it. I was grateful that I had not pressed the point.

The room was comfortable, fairly large by European standards and had a window looking out to the sea. The long stretch of rough sand beach behind the hotel was now completely abandoned. Mid-October was not the height of the tourist season and all the chairs, colorful umbrellas and tourists were gone for the season. The sea looked rather gray this day as the clouds projected their autumn bluster into it. The wind was brisk and the sea air bracingly cool. There would be no frolicking in the Mediterranean Sea on this trip, but that was not why we came in the first place. We were here to see the wonder of a city that rose eight hundred twenty feet above us on a mountain promontory, the majestic Taormina that had likely existed nearly a thousand years before the Greeks settled in Naxos next door at the foot of the mountain.

The road to Taormina from the hotel was steep and winding. This was expected. How else to get to the top? What was not expected was the marvel of engineering that met us at the halfway point. The mountain curved sharply to the left. The road continued straight. Just when you realize what is happening you are several hundred feet in the air with nothing but huge supporting columns and air holding up the highway. Then, what looks and feels like a lazy U turn brings you back to the mountain, the highway now clinging mercifully to the earth. Looking at this portion of the road from below and seeing it jut out beyond the mountain for what seemed an unreasonable distance brought back memories of all the stories of Italian highway collapses due to poor construction. I would try to limit my use of this particular engineering oddity in the future.

Arriving by car at the entrance to the city, one quickly discovers that a tourist can only drive through a very small area and cannot park within the small city limits. This is a place for locals and parking is extremely limited. This is as it should be. Taormina is best discovered on foot. A quick u-turn and another dizzying drive over the suspended portion of the highway would bring us to a parking structure several levels deep and at this time of year more than half empty. After parking the car, we found the stairs that we assumed would lead us to the city. Three short flights up merely brought us to the top of the parking structure. After some wandering, we then found the real stairs that would usher us up the city-all two hundred eighty-two of them. Undeterred, we mounted the now abandoned stairs and worked our way to the top.

As we climbed this never-ending staircase, I noticed something strange. The stairs we were continually turning to the left. One flight up, left turn at the landing, another flight up, an-

rises majestically to the southwest. Movie stars, writers and Russian Tsars have frequented this city in the past, and its reputation as an elite retreat is well deserved. The views and the atmosphere however, are free for the taking. A tablecloth adorned with bright Sicilian flowers of blue and gold with impossibly green leaves was a purchase that would serve us for many years and would always prompt Sicilian stories to tell our friends.

While we certainly could have lingered longer in the shops, I had something else in mind. There was an old fortress here rising some five hundred feet above the town. I had seen the crenelated walls of this Saracen castle in pictures and longed to see them and touch them for myself. A strenuous, hot and dry walk up a dirt path, then some wood and stone steps, and finally up a narrow trail, leads one to a small church on a promontory overlooking the city. As one walks this steep route, there are stone renditions of the stations of the cross until one finally reaches the top. At first glance, the church looks like a small stone house, the wooden door no larger than those found on modern apartments. The difference was the unmistakable cross above the entrance and the iron bars for a window. The church was surely ancient, and its thick walls were hewn from stone. It is actually carved into the massive rock structure, and I later learned that it dates from about 1640, or at least that is the day it was founded by Abbot Francesco Raineri. This cave like structure probably existed long before this date although it is clear that interior improvements were done by hand. Legend has it that a young shepherd boy was caught in a terrible lightning storm and believed that he and his flock was about to perish when a beautiful lady dressed in blue came to him and beckoned for him to wait out the storm in the cave. He and his entire flock was found safe after the storm passed, and his vision of the Madonna became the stuff of Catholic legend. As word traveled of the miracle, crowds of believers began to come to see this place where a miracle had occurred. Not to be left out, the bishop of Taormina also went to the cave and the Santuario della Madonna della Rocca was born.

Alas, on our arrival the door was locked, and no amount of pushing and pulling was about to move it. I wondered at my bad luck on choosing a day or perhaps a time when the church was not admitting visitors. It was late in the afternoon, and I would later learn that the door is locked after 12:30 p.m. in the winter. I suppose I could have looked that up before beginning the steep climb, but where is the adventure in that? I struggled to see through the iron bars on the window but was prevented from seeing anything beyond a glimpsing exploration of this wonder as darkness prevailed inside. The ceiling is roughhewn rock and the church appeared to be a large hollowed out cave of a structure. I could make out a whitewashed arch or two with painted decorations, but the darkness was unforgiving. The Santuario della Madonna della Rocca would keep its secrets on this day.

From the overlook, Taormina beckoned below, and beyond it the sea shimmered a deep blue. I could see the clustered roofs of the buildings and to one side the famous greco-roman amphitheater. It was from this overlook that one could appreciate the size and scope of the city built on a plateau overlooking the Ionian Sea. If one were to look up from Taormina to this spot, a large cross, lighted at night, would be visible from below. It was erected in 1930 overlooks the town and seemingly gives its blessing. We lingered here awhile both to catch our breath after the climb and to wonder at the view and the solitude found here. There was no other person in sight.

Undaunted by my failure to see the interior of the church, I located another stone and dirt path leading up to an iron gate beyond which was the Saracen castle. I climbed to the gate and began fumbling with the lock hoping it was open and wondering if I could get around this obstacle. One side of the path was a steep mountain, the other side a seemingly treacherous slope of loose dirt and blocking the way a twelve foot iron fence and gate. Suddenly, a voice reached my ears from far below. "Signore, il castello est siempre chiuso!" An old man, perhaps the caretaker was shouting to me from the path I had taken. While

have resulted in reconstructed columns and other structures from the original stones. Of the 45 original columns, only four and a half stand today. These are beautifully framed by the remnants of what are likely Roman brick walls on either side of the theater. Large pieces of other columns, whose bases stand at regular intervals waiting for their turn at reconstruction, lie on their sides as if struck down in battle during a war between the ancient Greek Gods. There are three arched entryways at the rear of the amphitheater, and one can imagine hordes of citizens streaming in to watch a spectacular performance while perched on the ancient stone gallery. The marble facing of the rear wall is long gone, no doubt suffering the same fate as the Roman colosseum wall coverings, removed and reused in some other ancient projects during a time when the theater was in disuse.

The legendary acoustics of this amphitheater can be heard to this day. I asked my wife to sit on the last row of stone benches in the center of the theater while I made my way down the thirty odd rows of stone benches to where the stage would have been far below. I stood atop one of the large stone blocks, in retrospect somewhere I probably should not have been. From here, I could see where the 5,400 spectators would have been looking down to the stage. In what I imagined to be a theatrical voice, I recited from Shakespeare's Hamlet: "To be or not to be? That is the question." I imagine this exact phrase has been broadcast by many thousands of other tourists over time, but I simply could not resist. My wife enthusiastically waved her arms signaling that she could hear me. I felt guilty at not saying something from a Greek or Roman play but, sadly, my repertoire seems limited.

This grand ancient place is still in use for modern jazz concerts, operatic endeavors and rock concerts. Unfortunate white plastic chairs have been set up on the lower tier to accommodate additional people. While the symmetry of the theater was maintained, the juxtaposition of modern plastic and ancient stone is jarring to the senses. I imagine the day, perhaps a thousand years from now, when the plastic chairs have long since melted into the earth from the heat of Etna's future fury and a new crop of archeologists uncover this magnificent site once again. The ancient Greeks and Romans will be rediscovered in stone, and we will not be evident at all.

It was disappointing that we were unable to see any performances in this magnificent place. The summer had ended and with it the promise of perfect acoustics and a date with the past faded, as did the warmth of the sun. A brisk wind blew in from the sea, and we retreated into town seeking the shelter and the warmth of the Sicilian people.

Now being thoroughly immersed in island life Italian Style, I was determined to continue the adventure on another

CHAPTER XIII
Sardinia

There was an island, we were told, where the interior was once ruled by bandits and roamed by shepherds. The culture was decidedly not Italian, and the food was still open pit roasted meats with unusual spices. The northeast of the island, I knew, had been taken over by the luxury tourism of the rich and famous, the "see and must be seen" crowd of recent fame and fortune. Villas, resorts and discos abound. So with no real planning except an idea to stay away from these more recent developments and a sudden burst of curiosity, the allure of the unknown was sufficient to make me buy tickets and cross the Tyrrhenian Sea from the Italian mainland to Sardinia.

To describe this trip as going to another part of Italy would be woefully inadequate. The language is nothing like Italian. The people are perhaps descended from the Lydians, another ancient civilization about which little is understood. There are mounded, circular tombs that can be seen rising up from the landscape, some explored others undisturbed. There are stone fortress-like towers on hilltops that are said to date from 1500 BC called Nuraghi. There are more than seven thousand of these scattered across the island. Some are small and some are monumental in size. Many are unguarded and able to be partially explored on foot if you ignore the signs indicating that trespassing is forbidden.

The landscape is harsh, dry and mountainous in the interior. It seems that even the Romans could not fully subdue these people, despite occupying the island for over 650 years. The Romans called the interior of Sardinia "Barbaria," the Barbarian land. Tribal groups of Sardinian people kept the Romans in fear of their lives if they ventured from the more coastal areas. Sardinia suffered a similar fate as Sicily, being invaded and ruled by successive waves of outsiders. The Romans, the Vandals, the Byzantines, the Moors, the Berbers, the Genoese and the Pisans all had their turns as well as the Aragonese and even the Sicilians themselves. It wasn't until the mid 1800s that the Sardinians were incorporated into the Kingdom of Italy. Its communal lands were abolished, its forests were cut down to provide the North of Italy with lumber. Several separatist groups emerged over the years and bombing campaigns were not unusual in the name of an independent Sardinia. The people of the interior are still viewed with some trepidation by the governmental authorities in the cities. Tales of banditry on the rural highways abound even if mostly untrue. While we were there, we never witnessed any acts of violence and were the recipients of many acts of kindness. Even the sheep, of which there are over four million on the island, seemed not to mind as they were herded around our car as we remained stopped in wonder on the road to the interior.

Cagliari and the surrounding area of the capital is a city of some 430,000 people. It is a bustling commercial port whose main street is littered with many restaurants, fashionable squares, and espresso cafes, chic and not so chic shops, and we decided rather quickly that we would forsake this artificial urban paradise for a look at more natural and rural areas of the island. Some brief conversations with a few locals was enough reason head west to a town called Villisimius, which we were assured was a beautiful seaside vacation spot and very much an up and coming destination currently known only to locals.

Before leaving, I purchased what I still find to be a fascinating book. It is a cookbook of Sardinian specialties. What sets this book apart is that every recipe handwritten in three languages: Sardinian, Italian and English. What fascinates me is that the recipe in Sardinian takes up two full pages of which I can read nothing; in Italian one page which I can see is quite abbreviated; and in English one paragraph mixing ingredients with the most rudimentary cooking instructions. The book has a cardboard cover and thick pages. I still find myself pouring over the Sardinian pages trying to figure out what exacting information must be being imparted to the truly Sardinian cook.

After a winding drive of two hours, we spotted a stunning bay below our mountain highway. Villisimius turned out to be beautiful, primitive, and quite touristic. There is just one street, some several hundred yards from the sea, populated by shops selling beachwear and Sardinian tourist trinkets. There was no real architecture to the buildings, and it was hot and dry as we walked the length of the street. Up on a hill, and overlooking the bay, was a double row of newly built and half-built condominiums, all for sale. There were several small hotels and we found ourselves in one of them a mere 100 yards from the beach. The beach, however, was stunning. The warm, knee deep water seemed to stretch forever toward the horizon. The water was crystal clear, and the sandy bottom was rippled as if reflecting the gentle lapping of these calm waters. There was a small cafe ten yards from the water with cold, white wines fit for a summer's day. I took a glass down to the water's edge and bathed my feet in the warmth of the sea while sipping the nectar of the Gods. Other than the beach, there was little of interest here. The restaurants were serviceable but not memorable. The views were outstanding and mesmerizing. Long walks in knee deep water while wearing a wide brimmed hat became the go-to activity during our brief stay at this idyllic seaside spot.

Once again, we had heard of another town that promised another adventure. Porto was a small beachside town that boast-

have ever had to pleasure to consume. Apparently, while we were talking, an octopus had been cooking in the kitchen. It was now brought to the table with an assortment of condiments, sauces and breads. We ate greedily and happily along with our host who occasionally would retreat to the kitchen to retrieve another delectable dish for our delight. A fish stew, a whole fish crusted in salt, a plate of mollusks, and unending wines were presented and we all enjoyed a most memorable meal.

When it was over, and I was wondering how I would ever walk to the car, our host began shaking my hand and bidding us farewell with tears in his eyes. I gently reminded him we had not paid for the meal whereupon he began to insist that we were his guests, and he would not be taking money from new found friends. This generosity was striking, and I was moved with his sincerity. However, now it was my turn to insist that if I could not pay then I would leave a gift for his dutiful staff who had worked on our behalf at an inopportune time of the day. He finally agreed to write down some meager prices and presented a bill for less than 50 euros for everything including the wine. Seeing my shock at the amount, he grabbed the bill and said, "Oh, I am sorry, it's too much" and started to discount it further. I laughed as one can with a friend and assured him that to the contrary, it was too little. I paid 100 euros. As we said our final goodbyes, he tore the flap off of a cardboard box and scribbled the words "Su Gogolone" on it. He pressed this into my hand and told us that since we had no real destination, we should go to this restaurant in the center of the island and near to the town of Nouro. He spoke of it as is it were a mythical place. I promised to go there and we took our long goodbyes and cheek kisses out to the parking lot where we lingered for another ten minutes. He seemed sad for us to leave him and as we drove away I could see him waving to us in the parking lot. It is an encounter I will never forget.

CHAPTER XIV
Su Gogolone

We drove into the town of Nouro not knowing exactly where this restaurant was located. Nouro turned out to be a very gritty, industrial town of warehouses, rundown buildings and, from what I could see, a single gas station on the main road. There are sharp granite mountains directly behind the town that jut straight up from the earth and prematurely block the sun in the afternoon. When we arrived, it was late and darkness was descending. I stopped the first person I saw and asked if he knew where this restaurant was located. I was directed further down the road to the town of Oliana, a farming community with vineyards and rolling fields of green. Two older Sardinian women walking in the street were kind enough to wave us toward the correct direction, an unmarked, dirt road. Towards the end of this road we came upon a cluster of blue and white, small dwellings and a one larger building that we soon discovered was a hotel. A lucky find for us, or so I thought, since the hour was getting late.

As we pulled into the parking lot, the sky opened and a torrential rain began. We ran to the hotel and arrived looking like wet animals, hair streaming and disheveled. At the desk, I

ushered into a beautifully rustic adjacent building, probably a newly renovated old barn that had four rooms built into it. There were bathrooms in a separate building, one full large bath and two smaller sink and toilet rooms. In desperate need of a shower, I took my towel and headed to the full bath. Upon entering, I could see that someone had laid out all of their personal hygiene items on the shelf and had clothing hanging from the towel racks. I closed the door and proceeded to move the clothes a safe distance from the water flow and entered the shower. A moment later there was a furious pounding on the door and from what minuscule German I could understand, I gathered that whomever was pounding thought I was in his exclusive bathroom. Apparently the concept of a shared master bath was erased by the discovery that no-one else had rented a room in the remodeled barn. I ignored the commotion and finished with my shower. Afterward, as I retreated to our room, I saw the owner and explained what had happened. I last saw him that night having a conversation with the German guests explaining that the full bath was for everyone and no one was relegated to the sink and toilet rooms which were for immediate convenience. The next morning, as we were wakened by the sound of sheep being herded past our window, we found that all of the personal belongings had been removed from the bathroom shelf. Still, the Germans never smiled at us for the rest of our stay.

Dinner was offered as a part of our accommodation and included in the basic price. We, however, had reservations at Su Gogolone. We headed back to the blue and white hotel and took a good look at our surroundings. There was a room full of Sardinian puppets, some almost full size in one large room. I would later learn that these were part of the animalistic yet somehow Catholic religious processions that marked the religious holidays. On such days, the entire town participated in a rural procession through the fields, and the town dressed in full, masked animal costumes with large bells hanging from their belts. The procession was led by the local priest intoning in Latin and carrying a large cross. Easter was the largest of these processions, and I marveled at the fact that these people would set aside their own lives to become something ancient and awe inspiring for a brief moment in time. I made sure to buy a miniature puppet which I carried on the plane much to the chagrin of my fellow passengers who had to put up with what looked like an upright sheep staring at them for the entire flight.

Through another room I could see the kitchen with a large roaring fire along one wall. Various animals were flayed out on double skewers and leaned into the fire at an angle. Periodically, a very sweaty kitchen worker would turn each skewer so that the animal cooked evenly. The wood crackled and glowed red in the night. The smoke escaped through a hole in the roof. This was a throwback to the old ways of cooking in Sardinia when shepherds and bandits alike would cook by open fires in the night air. I felt the pangs of history as I watched the spectacle unfold. I could imagine being hunched over a fire in the open mountain air along with my comrades in arms as we devoured whatever the surrounding countryside had provided. My reverie was broken by the host's announcement that our table was ready. White tablecloths took the place of the forest floor and my wife and I sat down for what would prove to be a magnificent meal.

When it comes to brains, I generally feel that we should use them and not necessarily eat them. This night, however, brought to the table an assortment of pastry puffs with what I would later discover was sheep brain with savory seasonings. It was sublime. My wife was having none of it. She finds the thought of eating this delicacy as disgusting as she finds the smell of lamb, another favorite of mine. Oh well, more for me. One course followed upon another, each a marvel of thoughtful preparation: spices of myrtle, mint, juniper berries and the flavor of the mountains. We ate for what seemed like hours savoring every morsel. I could not resist ordering the roasted lamb that I had seen cooking earlier, and it did not disappoint: Succulent, tender, interestingly spiced and perfectly roasted. Looking back on this night, we both recall it as one of the best meals we have ever eaten. Even now, I can almost taste it. But reverie only takes one so far, and we had a grand destination to discover. The next day, a short airplane ride would bring us the eternal city of Rome.

CHAPTER XV

Roma

How can one describe Rome? The seat of the Roman Empire for centuries? The home of the Holy See and the Vatican? The stuff of legends, true and fanciful, and the most amazing concentrated collection of open-air ancient sites anywhere in the world. To be sure, we had been here before, spending a week here and there over the years. This time, I rented a flat for a month on the ancient street of Governo del Vecchio, a stone's throw from Piazza Navona and the Fountain of the Four Rivers. We were just across from an old clock tower which would serve as our landmark and guide home over the next thirty days.

We arrived with bags in tow and were dropped directly in front of the apartment by our very efficient taxi driver. The large doors, easily twenty feet high, were open and we entered a courtyard strewn with parked cars. There was a man sitting in a small office who greeted us and explained that the owner would be there shortly to explain the rental. We were shown the lift, given a key and a few moments later we were in our fourth-floor accommodation, a two bedroom flat with a kitchen, bathroom, living room and a dining area. The owner arrived, a middle aged woman, who for the next half hour talked non-stop about the apartment, the area, the restaurants, the cleaning fee, the maid if we wanted her, the use of the keys for the oversized door after hours and the operation of the washer, stove, coffeemaker and windows. She deposited two sets of keys in a small tray by the front door and, with that, she was gone. The laughter that followed was impossible to hold back as we attempted to recall even the smallest bit of the wealth of information she had imparted. Luckily, I had operated windows before and there were several cards from local establishments left by others as silent recommendations for dining.

Renting over the internet has provided both wonderful and slightly strange accommodations over the years. For instance, the bed in our Roman flat was just that—flat, hard and unforgiving. If you like sleeping on the floor, you would love this bed. I took all of the pillows from the couch in the living room, including the cushions designed for sitting, and attempted to make a softer place to rest my weary body. The spaces between the cushions would open during the night in an attempt to swallow me and many nights were spent fighting a valiant battle with them until, quite exhausted, I would give in to slumber. My wife's small stature was an asset for her as she could sleep quite well on just two cushions. Later, seeing her sleeping soundly reminded me that it is sometimes hard to be happy for someone when you yourself are uncomfortable. I resisted the urge to wake her and then pretend I was sleeping.

After studying a map of the city, I was ready to strike out on an adventure. We headed down Via Julia, a remarkably straight road that is lined with chic shops. Via Julia has beautiful palaces, museums and churches on both sides of the street. It was built in the sixteenth century by Pope Julius II as a way to get directly to the Vatican without taking windingly inconvenient roads. As a result, it is straight, wide and just far enough from the normal tourist sites to be quiet and uncrowded. Those who have a love of history, as I do, should spend some time discovering its beauty. At the far end of the street, the Farnese family, one of the most influential and ancient families of Rome, had a palace here. When they sought to connect it to the Villa Farnese, on the other side of the river, they commissioned none other than Michelangelo to build an arch across the road and a bridge to the villa. Sadly, the bridge was never built and the project was abandoned sometime later, but the magnificent arch remains. As we passed under it, I could see thick, green ivy that had claimed half of it and no doubt would claim the remainder by summer's end. Nearby, there is a bathtub looking fountain about twenty-five feet long and six feet wide which is said to have been occasionally filled with wine for the Farnese family festivities, the wine flowing freely in place of the water. The

very good sign, and we entered. I was wearing a typical tourist tee shirt that boldly stated the word ROMA on the front. Immediately upon entering, a waiter gestured to me and loudly asked in English, "Are you looking for Rome?" I replied in Italian, "Yes, where is it?" He answered with a twinkle in his eye and said, "Ecco la!" Here it is! As we were ushered to a table and sat down, he asked if we had been walking the city all day. I said yes. He told me the streets of Rome were always dusty and I could not do anything but agree that indeed they were dusty. Just then he produced a large bowl of water and set it in front of me. By now, everyone was watching this bit of theater playing out. He asked me to place my hands behind my back and bend slightly over the bowl. He smiled broadly and said, "Prego." I did as he asked. He then produced a piece of soap and began to dip it into the water and scrub my face and beard while singing at the top of his lungs. This accomplished, he handed me a towel and I dried myself while laughing heartily. The bowl was replaced by a plate of sausage, pepperoni, salami, bread, cheese and a large knife. We proceeded to enjoy the feast. The patrons at this establishment all enjoyed this spectacle and laughed along with us, gasped and shook their heads. A bottle of wine appeared at the table, compliments of our neighbor diners who let us know in language and gesture that we were welcome here. We enjoyed the warm company of our fellow diners and the staff. I tried to make conversation, at least as much as my limited Italian would allow, and felt like we had made a connection with these wonderfully playful people. Complimentary grappa and limoncello followed a marvelous meal.

After dinner, we found our way back to the clock tower apartment, changed clothes and headed out for our evening passegiata. Piazza Navona beckoned and we could hear the sounds of a bustling square even as we approached.

CHAPTER XVI
Piazza Navona

There is a storied ice cream parlor in Piazza Navona called Tre Scalini. The tartufo ice cream is legendary and since by now all guide books have included this little gem, the place is packed with locals and tourists alike. The small ice cream shop has grown over the years and now boasts a full and quite large restaurant fronting the piazza. A group of noisy Italian children ranging in age from perhaps seven to twelve were all impatiently waiting for their ice cream. My wife and I joined in the line and enjoyed the night's summer air and festive atmosphere. I was suddenly struck by a silence that was as disturbing as the previous shrieking of the children had been just moments before. Looking to the curb, I saw all fifteen of the children, ice cream cones in hand, silently licking their treats with serious concentration. It seems that this ice cream had the power to subdue these young and wild beasts even if only for the few minutes it took to finish the cones. We laughed at the sight and lack of sound . I desperately wanted to capture this sight in a photograph and, like every other tourist, I was camera ready. The children looked up for the picture but never once lost their concentration on the ice cream, trying to lick it before it melted or dripped into their laps. The memory of this night is delicious.

Piazza Navona is what is left of the stadium and circus that the Emperor Domitian built in 86AD. Standing in the center, one can make out the oblong design seemingly fit for chariot races, mock sea battles and jousts. One has to imagine the stadium seats rising to the sides of the track. Now, the seats are gone in favor of some very expensive apartments, a ring of restaurants and the grand Pamphili Palace housing the Museum of Rome at one end.

In the center of Piazza Navona is Bernini's Fountain of the Four Rivers, a marriage of four sculptures depicting the four known rivers of the ancient world with a towering obelisk, recovered from the Circus Maxentius, rising toward the heavens. On the top is a dove holding an olive branch, a symbol of peace. Each statue has plants and animals thought to be from the river areas as well as palm trees, lions and horses that seem to guard the rivers. Pope Innocent X had commissioned the great architect Bernini after some controversy since this artist was not in favor after the last pope refused to recognize his genius. We can be thankful that artistic reason prevailed as the result is one of the most enchanting squares in all of Rome. Bernini's design was faithfully executed by his students, all master sculptors in their own right. The Nile River is depicted as a statue of a muscular man with a covering over his head to symbolize the mystery of the origins of the river. The Ganges, representing Asia, is pictured as a partially reclining oarsman to symbolize the ability to travel the length of the river by boat. The Danube, depicted by a statue with a laurel wreath on its head symbolizes the primacy of Europe and touches the papal coat of arms. The Rio de la Plata, with a garter on one leg, sits on a pile of presumably silver coins symbolizing the wealth thought to exist in the Americas. The fountain is wonderfully lighted at night with the water and the marble glinting and the light and shadows playing the surfaces of the sculpture that continually change as one walks around this truly monumental work.

Naturally, tour guides have made up stories to delight tourists and explain some features of the fountain. The raised arm of the figure representing the Rio de la Plata seems to be trying to protect itself from the imminent collapse of the Church of Agnes in Agone just a few dozen feet away. That church, which now holds classical and baroque music concerts throughout the summer, was designed by the rival architect Borromini. A quick check of the dates of construction reveal the Fountain of the Four Rivers was unveiled in 1651, while construction of the Church of Agnes in Agone was only just begun in 1652. In spite of the truth, guides happily tell their stories, tourists are delighted at some perceived inside gossip from the 1600s, and no one gets hurt. Besides, the rivalry was real and well known and perhaps that is the point after all.

The many restaurants in the piazza are more expensive than they should be. It is not surprising as this is the favored gathering place of tourists, locals, minstrels, jugglers, artists and the youth of Rome. Tables had been set up on over 50% of the piazza on several of the nights we were there. An international bridge tournament was being featured. We learned that many events were held here during the summer months. The other half of the piazza gave itself over to artists, lovers, singers and people like us who just wanted to connect with this pleasant way of life. Mercifully, the authorities do not allow cars in this piazza, and it remains one of the charms of Rome at any hour.

CHAPTER XVII
The Spanish Steps

At the foot of Via Veneto, that winding, tree lined street of overly expensive restaurants stretching from the Borghese Gardens to Piazza Barberini, one can find a heavily trafficked square with two Bernini fountains, one in the center and one to the side.

The larger center one is the Fontana del Tritone. It is an imposing monument to the Barberini family of the 1600s. Triton seems to be sitting on a large clamshell being held aloft by four large fish, water gushing overhead from an upraised conch above them. Triton appears to be blowing the water out of the conch into the air. The fish look angry, and their mouths are open and menacing. A papal crown and keys rest safely within the larger clamshell, and three prominent Barberini Bees, the family crest, are centered on a scroll. There is a metal rail surrounding the fountain that can provide a momentary resting spot but the square itself is not very inviting due to the traffic whizzing by at all hours. There is no shade or shelter from the weather here. A large hotel sits at the top of the square, appropriately named Hotel Bernini, and a national art gallery occupies the old palace of the Barberini family. Still this piazza is a historic site and a testament to the power and influence of Cardinal Barberini and his family.

The smaller Bernini fountain sits to one side almost hidden from view by parked cars, trees and signs. This one is at the corner of Via Veneto. The fountain is faithful in its design to its benefactors, the   Barberinis, showcasing the three bees of the family crest and extolling the virtues and greatness of the Barberini Pope Urban VIII in 1644. The inscription, in Latin, announces that the water in this fountain is for the benefit of the animals and people of Rome. A fitting gift to the people of Rome that, unfortunately, was bone dry on the day I chose to go there. It was hot, and I could only imagine the refreshment that would have come from the ice-cold water normally spouting from it. I would settle for bottled water from the market nearby.

At the lower end of the Piazza, there is a small, somewhat narrow street that runs uphill for about a quarter mile. This is Via Sistina and it leads to the Church of Trinita dei Monti at the top of the Spanish Steps. It passes a few interesting restaurants and shops and finally opens onto the entrance of the church. Most ignore the church, a shame, and turn their back to it in order to gaze at the expanse of the Spanish Steps below. This staircase, 135 steps by my count, was built to connect the Spanish Embassy to the church in 1725. Financed by the French, who owned the church, and built by the Spanish who controlled the land of the Spanish embassy, it has become the gathering place for the youth of Rome and more than a few tired tourists who take respite from their walks by sitting here for a few minutes to a few hours. If you are lucky enough to be here during the spring, the steps are adorned with pink and red azaleas which makes them look truly romantic. If you are here some other time, the steps appear as a somewhat severe, sun drenched expanse of stairs divided into three sections with the center wider than the two side aisles. Crowds of students, tourists and a few locals make the atmosphere festive and the walking interesting.

This is one of the best people watching places in Rome. Take a seat about halfway up and enjoy the view. I have heard that eating lunch here is forbidden but enforcement is lax, and nearly everyone has a bottled water and is munching on something. The conversations range from the disappointed tourist, to the romantic couple, to the excitement of the youth scattered in groups. Looking down one sees a fountain of a boat at the foot of the stairs. This is again a Bernini masterpiece, Fontana della Barcaccia, said to have been ordered by the Pope to be constructed on this spot as a reminder of the 1598 Tiber River flood that brought a real boat to this very spot when a particularly severe storm caused the river to overflow its banks and invade the city. A bride, dressed in her very fashionable and very full gown was gingerly walking across the small tongue in the fountain that leads to two water spouts, one on either side of the boat. Her dress was gathered into her hands, and she wore a broad smile on her face. Her new husband dutifully removed his shoes and braved the cold water to support her all to the cheers from the crowd who were lucky enough to be spectators to this triumph of love. The bride drank from the fountain, and the crowd roared its approval, surely a perfect start to a long and fruitful marriage. I marveled at the thought that the water here came from the Aqua Vergine, an aqueduct built in 19BC.

To the right of the Spanish Steps, as one faces them, is the house of Keats and Shelly, the English romantic poets who called this place home for a short time. Keats tragically came to this beautiful place for the weather, hoping to cure or at least improve his tuberculosis. He died a slow and painful death at age twenty-five but was said to have been able to hear the water splashing in the fountain just outside. The window frames, doors, floors, walls and all the furniture were burned for public health reasons after his death. The museum, which is now open to the public, features a faithful replication of the era.

Beyond the Spanish Steps and the Bernini boat, one will find the most exquisite and expensive shopping district in Rome. The larger street directly in front of the fountain is Via Condotti. A more compact area of narrow streets line either side of this grand boulevard. Here one can find every brand name one can imagine. I stopped counting after reaching forty brands I recognized. About halfway down Via Condotti there is a beautiful cafe, Antico Caffe Greco. It is a grand belle epoch style cafe that is said to have existed since 1760, at least that is what the sign on the building says. With a gilded interior that instantly transports you back to that golden age. It is the perfect respite from the hoards of tourist groups, shoppers and gawkers that fill this area in summer. Waiters attend every patron in tux and tails carrying silver trays. Art is on every wall. Mirrors reflect patrons, art and staff alike. Statues abound in every corner. Small round tables line the walls, and the romantic age comes alive, with espresso, spirits and pastries. There are several rooms here and even a library room full of antique bookcases overflowing with ancient tomes. Just by sitting here, one cannot help but be swept up in the aura of the age, feeling at once grand and content. Gazing at the surroundings one can feel the spirits of Byron, Keats, Goethe, Stendhal and others who have spent their time here and for a few brief moments join them in convivial community.

CHAPTER XVIII
The Villa Borghese

Passing through Piazza del Popolo, the impossibly large square with an ancient Egyptian obelisk in the center and walking to the right will lead to stairs that take one to the Pincio park which in turn leads to the Borghese gardens, a green lung of the city studded with small cafes, museums, gardens and statuary. It is easy to get lost here although that is not a bad thing. There are signs pointing the way to various landmarks and roads scattered throughout the park. At the far edge, the Villa Borghese stands as a shrine to magnificent art. Arriving without a reservation will result in either a several hours wait or a ticket for the following day. The museum restricts the number of visitors at any given time which makes for a very pleasant visit.

On the day we arrived, it was threatening rain. We had arrived early and were told to wait until the time on our ticket, an hour later. With nothing to do, we decided to stroll the grounds on the exterior. There are a number of statues arranged around a courtyard, and I dutifully walked to each one to get a better look. In one place, the statue was missing and only the marble base remained. Naturally, I deftly jumped onto the pedestal and struck a pose fitting for a Roman and waited for my wife to take a picture. My internal sense of urgency, prompted by some dirty looks of others in the area was apparently not shared by my wife. Perhaps seeking the perfect angle, better light, or a more interesting framed background, I stood for what felt like an eternity holding a pose that looked like a crazy person in profile on one leg holding aloft an invisible jug of wine. When the smile had run away from my face, I finally heard the merciful click of the camera. As I dismounted my perch, I could hear her voice saying, "Wait, just one more!" I think not. Let me explain. Whenever I pose for what I think will be a charming memory of perhaps a silly moment in time, it is then that my wife becomes an artiste with the camera. In more normal pictures, she waits until I have waited so long that I am now speaking, hands raised to the sky, with a look of incredulity before the magic click. When the pose is truly silly, somewhat embarrassing and usually illegal, or at least insensitive to situation, that is when the truly artistic side of my wife comes to the fore and time stands still while she searches for the perfect moment which apparently only comes after I start walking away. On return from a vacation, I can't believe how many walking shots of me were taken with a look on my face that says, "What is taking you so long?" Of course, I understand this is my flaw, not hers. I seem to be in more of a hurry for no particular reason, and my Italian background makes me express myself when perhaps I should not. At any rate, she tolerates me and we have more fun together than apart. It has been that way for as long as I can remember.

The clouds finally burst forth with a torrent of rain. Just as suddenly, a veritable army of umbrella sellers appeared from nowhere hawking their now essential wares. I bought a garishly colored plaid umbrella for three times a normal price. Beggars cannot be choosy. The umbrella seller immediately disappeared. I opened the umbrella just as a gust of wind struck with considerable force inverting the umbrella and nearly tearing it from my hands. I managed to get it back into shape with one side now irreparably damaged and hanging down. I used this sad excuse for an umbrella for exactly ten minutes whereupon, the sun came out, the wind stopped, and the trash receptacle became the graveyard of several tourist umbrellas. The umbrella sellers appeared again, but this time they had plastic water bottles and hats, all for a good price. I decided to forego any other purchases and entered the Villa Borghese a little damp but undeterred.

The Galleria Borghese is a wonderland of sculpture by the likes of Canova and Bernini, paintings by Caravaggio, Titan, Reubens and others. After entering the magnificent palatial mansion through a small door in the enter and checking in at the ticket counter, you will have exactly two hours to complete your exploration. Visits are timed to keep the crowds manageable. The Borghese family was a storied and powerful line of cardinals, lawyers, church officials and even a pope, Paul V. It was one of these, a certain Cardinal Scipione Borghese, who was responsible for this magnificent art collection. His private, seventeenth century villa provides the perfect setting for this artistic display. There are a number of truly moving and emotional sculptures here. Bernini's David with his jaw set and muscles tensed is breathtaking. Likewise, the mystical Apollo and Daphne are captured in stone just at the moment when Daphne is transforming into a laurel tree as Apollo reaches out to possess her. Her fingers turning to leaves, her feet to roots and her body to the truck of the tree. Beholding this masterpiece makes one appreciate the ancient Greeks competing for the prize of a laurel wreath, a symbol of victory. Entering another room brings one face to face with the sculpted Rape of Proserpina, another Bernini wonder. Proserpina's futile resistance and sorrowful look were captured in a way that makes one weep. Yet another room holds Canova masterworks. Pauline Bonaparte reclines on a couch, as lifelike as one can imagine. The gallery allows one to get very close to each work of art, to study the line and sweep of each piece. Two hours passes quickly, but perhaps that is the right amount of time to spend among these spectacular artistic endeavors. I left with visions of the ancient world swirling in my head, quite overwhelmed by the emotional and moving experience.

Outside, a street to the left will lead you back to the Spanish Steps by way of the church Trinita dei Monti. Even entering the crowd of tourists and locals on the steps could not dull the euphoria of the artistic experience that is the Galleria Borghese.

CHAPTER XIX
Castel Sant'Angelo

On the Vatican side of the Tiber River is an absolutely gigantic, drum shaped monster of a building with a statue of Michael the Archangel on top. From a distance it looks like a heavily fortified rectangular fortress with a large round structure rising from the center. There is a bridge adorned with ten statues of angels, the Ponte Sant'Angelo, leading to the opposite bank of the Tiber, which is where I was standing trying to take picture without tourists in it, a fool's errand at any time of the year. Thinking I would try again later, I turned around and struck out in the direction of a certain shop my wife had seen and wanted to revisit. I was much too proud to consult a map, my Italian heritage making me feel as though I could navigate this errand without difficulty. The streets of this neighborhood are not laid out in any discernible pattern. I followed one street after another very sure I was headed in the direction of Piazza Navona. I was convinced that the particular shop I was looking for was just around the next corner. Imagine my surprise when I looked up to see the imposing Castel Sant'Angelo once again directly in front of me. I was again at the foot of the bridge as though I had not moved at all. Undeterred, with my wife saying something about a map, I again turned to face the town, my back to the river and again began to walk toward Piazza Navona. I was careful this time to navigate by looking at signs trying to go opposite the direction of the Castle. I deliberately took sharp turns creating a grid pattern in my mind where none existed on the ground. Finally, at the last turn and feeling a little triumphant, we emerged onto the main street. Castel Sant'Angelo loomed ahead beckoning to us. How it got there, I will never understand. I stared in disbelief as my wife began to laugh a not so soft derisive laugh at my precision navigation. I swallowed what little pride I had left and announced that we were going to visit the castle. I think I heard the ten statuary angels joining my wife in laughter.

Castel Sant'Angelo was a mausoleum originally built to honor and hold the remains of the Emperor Hadrian and his family. It was built in first half of the first century AD and has withstood the ravishes of time and mankind. It has been many things during its lifetime including a castle, a fortress, the papal residence, military barracks and finally the museum you can visit today. It has been the resting place of Roman Emperors through Caracalla who died in 212 AD and inhabited since then by popes and prisoners alike. The Romans converted it into part of the defensive walls of the city. It was the scene of looting by the Visogoths in 515 AD, and later Papal looting in the fourteenth and fifteenth centuries. The Visigoths were trying to destroy Rome as a power while the popes were trying to adorn the Vatican with stone columns and marble statues taken from this once pagan monument. One can only imagine what it would look like with its original marble coverings, columns and statuary. It has suffered the same fate as the venerable Colluseum, losing its exterior covering and adornment such that the existing shell shows the earthwork and brick beneath.

The addition of the statue of Michael the Archangel is said to be from a vision of Pope Gregory in 590 AD when the angel was said to have appeared as a sign that the plague was to be lifted from the city. A less charitable explanation was that Pope Gregory was trying to wipe out pre-Christian religion and so had this most Christian symbol placed above the once pagan mausoleum. Either way, the statue is magnificent and glints above the castle in all its glory.

One enters the castle through an enormous gate. The drawbridge which once existed here is sadly no longer. Upon entering, a corridor leads to a long ramp which winds its way up the interior of the building. Ramps and a few stairs complete the journey to the next level. Along the way, several rooms and continuing excavations are visible but the opulence that was once here is gone and the remaining shell although imposing, is no longer a marvel of beauty. It remains a marvel of architecture and one can easily see the military application. Cannonballs are neatly stacked in the courtyard and the walls and guard posts can be visited through which one can view the city as it fans out below. On this upper level, there is a small cafe serving espresso and small bites to eat. If you are lucky enough, you can grab a table next to the castle wall overlooking the city. The wind drifts through the ancient openings and everything from St Peters to the mighty Tiber can be viewed for the cost of a cup of coffee.

We were told that there is a not so secret passageway leading from the Vatican to the castle. This is called the Passetto di Borgo. It is a covered walkway which protected popes from various invaders as they fled from the Vatican to the relative safety of the fortified castle. We were told that the passage had been used many times including by Pope Alexander VI, the famous Borgia Pope, who was fleeing Charles VIII and by Pope Clement VII in 1527 during another famous sack of Rome. Try as I might, I could never locate this passage and no one I asked seemed to know its location although everyone knew exactly what I was looking for. To this day, it has kept its secrets from me.

CHAPTER XX
Perugia and the Fairy Tale Castle

One of the pleasures of traveling without a defined itinerary is that it allows one to wander into places that might otherwise be bypassed by being more organized. Setting out from Rome in our rented Fiat and determined to head into the storied hill towns of Tuscany, the thought of semi-sweet, dark and luxurious chocolate seemed to cause the vehicle I was driving to follow the signs that pointed in the direction of Perugia. It was in this way that we found the Perugina Chocolate Factory and stopped to gather some "Baci," Italian for kisses, for the rest of our trip. The chocolate factory is now owned by Nestle, and the ubiquitous chocolate kisses are sold in virtually every store that sells candy. The factory is located in a rather gritty area of San Sisto, Perugia surrounded by other low slung, sinister looking, no nonsense factory buildings. Even so, the smell of chocolate begins at the road and permeates the parking lot. Following our noses, and salivating at the thought of melting one of these kisses in our mouths blotted out any bad feelings that the dismal landscape might have produced.

Upon entering the factory, I was reminded of the other constant to traveling without a designated itinerary, the last tour of the factory had already left the lobby and was ten minutes beyond our reach. Undeterred and mesmerized by the overwhelming smell of chocolate, I saw there were placards with explanations in English and Italian describing the process and some large windows overlooking some old chocolate making apparatus. We contented ourselves with these explanations and looked over the copper vats and other machinery that produced those wonderful kisses. Half an hour later, I made the inevitable purchase of too many chocolates, stuffed another sample in my mouth and stuttered out "grazie" around my delicious Baci. We headed for the car very contentedly.

Perugia is an Umbrian City known for its ancient Etruscan origins and its University that was apparently established in 1308. I know this because I have a hat that says so, purchased from a thoroughly reliable vendor in the city center. I did not intend to go to the city center. Let's just say that the road and signage led me there not completely unwillingly. On this occasion the "tutti le direzione" sign conspired with the "centro" sign, and we ended up in the opposite direction that I had intended. My intention was to find a storybook castle that had leapt off the pages of a book pointing out interesting places to stay in Italy. I did have the foresight to make an advance reservation for the castle and soon found myself on some small backroads in the town of Cenerente.

One would think that finding a storybook castle in the middle of a small village would be an easy feat. One would be wrong to make such an assumption. After passing the local gas station (two pumps and no attendant) for the third time, my wife made the seemingly wise suggestion that I stop and ask someone for directions. It is strange how that suggestion can go from being an affront to my masculinity and ability to figure out things, to a very reasonable alternative as the sun begins to set and the roads continually fail to deposit me in the right place.

I stopped at the gas station and wandered around for a few minutes until I found an older man walking on the road. In my best broken Italian, I asked him where the castle was located and explained that I had been looking for it for over an hour. He had a kindly face and a willingness to help. He simply pointed up the hill with his cane saying "ecco la, ecco la!" Indeed, as I turned my gaze upwards and toward the hill, I could clearly see the outlines of a crenelated castle wall that rose above the trees. I realized I had been traveling at the base of the hill, back and forth, hoping to run into the castle. The fact the castles were always built on the highest points of the land for better defenses somehow had escaped me in this last hour. I thanked our guide and got back in the car announced in my most matter of fact voice that, of course, I had found it. My wife smiled broadly but managed to stay quiet, which was no small feat, and which allowed me the feeling of a small victory over the gods of chaos and confusion. We both knew that without the old man's help we might still be driving all around a hill whose mystical castle was looking down at us wondering just how long it would take for us to look up.

Castello dell'Oscano looks like you would expect a castle to look like, minus the moat and drawbridge. As we approached, the evening sun bathed the walls in a golden light which made the castle look even more mythical than my imagination could conjure. In fact, it is a wholly rebuilt building having nothing to do with the original castle that was built on this site in the 1360s. Rather than being held by one or a few families over the years, this castle has had many different owners. In the 1600s a villa was built on the ruins of the old castle. It changed hands many times finally becoming the property of a lawyer who in 1895 sold it to Countess Ada Hungerford and Giuseppe Telfner. We learned the Countess had built her renaissance style residence over the site of what was either an old church or a hunting lodge and used it to accommodate her guests. Beneath the house was either a crypt or a stable for the horses. Sadly, we never saw it ourselves as others had rented the historic building and did not seem keen to have guests wandering through their lodgings. My guess is the residence was an old hunting lodge as it seems rather square with no room for a cemetery or other supportive structures. It's short distance from the castle would have made it a perfect place to stop with the horses, leave off the spoils of the hunt and get cleaned up before re-entering the castle. I have never tried to verify this preferring to leave it to my imagination. We were also told that the renovation and rebuilding of the castle under Telfner took over ten years and resulted in the architecturally medieval castle one can see today. It currently bills itself as a wedding destination and luxury vacation hotel. The only remaining remnant of the old castle I could find was a small arched structure on the road leading through a neglected vineyard. Its crumbled stone and overgrown walls are a testament to the forces of nature and the neglect of mankind.

The castle sits in the middle of a five hundred acre park and is comprised of three buildings, a farmhouse, the Villa Ada and the main castle itself. I had booked a room in the castle and was very pleased at the outward appearance of this fairytale structure. Standing in front of the castle, one almost expects to see archers standing between the spaces in the upper walls. The large wooden entrance door is crowned with a stone arch on top of which sits a beautifully designed Moorish window. The window is actually three windows placed next to each other and separated by narrow columns, which are, in turn, held within an arched enclosure. Ivy pours down the facade from the roof giving it an enchanted look. To the left and at a ninety-degree angle to the main facade is a portico consisting of three two story arches and a large balcony. At the end of this is a massive stone square tower that widens as it rises skyward and towers above the main building. The opposite end of the castle has a round turret style tower and there is yet another square tower on the other end. The forest rises to meet the castle walls and evergreen trees grace the surrounding area. The look is breathtaking and it is easy to see why many Italians get married here. The magical and enchanting castle grounds and buildings are the perfect setting for memorable pictures to share with friends.

Entering the castle through the large wooden door reveals an interior that does not disappoint. The center room is large with a wooden ceiling and massive chandelier. On the right is a wide wooden staircase that leads to the back wall where it is joined by a second staircase that ascends to the second level where the guest rooms are located. The main room has a nearly walk-in fireplace and large comfortable looking chairs, antique tables, ornate lamps and large upper windows, through which the last light of the day streamed in. As we walked up the stairs, we were met with the creaks and groans of old wood as the steps gave ever so slightly beneath our weight. There would be no sneaking down these stairs. The room had a high ceiling, an old amour, a double bed and several pictures on the walls.

From the window, one could see the forest and smell the freshness of the countryside. It was ideal, and I could not resist feeling slightly royal, even if I knew it was all make believe. The library had books dated from the 1700s which were available to see, hold and carefully turn pages of the past. We browsed through these Latin and French volumes to our delight. In the evening, a glass of port and dimly lighted lamps provided the perfect atmosphere.

A word about drinking port in a castle. It was late afternoon when my wife and I got the bright idea to have a glass of something while we perused the library. I sought out the only person around who turned out to be a waiter for the restaurant within the castle walls. I asked him for two glasses of port. He looked thoroughly surprised at my request. "Porto? Adesso?" I assured him he had heard me correctly, and he glanced toward the kitchen nervously. He then patiently explained with just a touch of condescension that port was for after dinner, and he wasn't sure he could get the bottle past the chef at this hour, who would surely object to this breech of protocol. However, he would try. My wife and I took our seats in the library and began to page through some ancient texts. A few minutes later, the waiter appeared with two glasses of port, shielding them with his body from the kitchen staff. He was relieved to have reached the library, and we were grateful for the drinks. No matter the time, it seemed appropriate to drink something like port when sitting in a castle with books a few hundred years old.

That next night we opted to eat at the castle restaurant. This restaurant was for castle guests only, and one had to reserve a place in the morning for the evening meal. Having done so, we were treated to a wonderful feast of flavors and smells. This was not a Michelin starred restaurant, far from it, but the setting, the crisp air of the evening, the baroque furnishings and the white table cloths in a magnificent dining hall all conspired to trick the senses into believing that the meal to be served would be one of the best in memory. Once again, the feeling of being royalty was irresistible and we allowed ourselves to be transported accordingly. Our meal was excellent, the wine was sublime, the conversation engaging and the atmosphere perfect. We lingered as long as we thought prudent and decided to take a short night time walk circumnavigating the castle.

As we walked along the stone walls, we passed the restaurant frontage and turned to walk along the side of the massive dining hall. There was a window positioned about four feet off the ground leading directly into the kitchen and through which we could smell the scent of the evening's dinner. At the window on the outside was a young man on a bicycle. The bicycle was old and had a basket attached to the front. The young man was leaning into the window conversing in hushed tones to an equally young woman who was clearly a kitchen helper of some sort. At first, I thought this was a lover's rendezvous, but as we got a little closer, I could see that packages of food were being passed out of the window and placed in the basket of the bicycle. We turned around and went back the way we came. I did not mention this to anyone. In my mind, I preferred to think that what we saw was an act of charity rather than an obvious theft. Having worked in restaurants for years, I knew better, but I didn't want to spoil the memory of this place with a more sordid picture of reality.

The following afternoon, we decided to mount the winding castle stairs to the roof. The view was magnificent. The view through the forest went on for miles. Rich greenery and rolling hills filled the view with the scents of fresh forest trees and grasses. As we were marveling at the view, I noticed an iron ladder attached to the rounded turret at the end of the roof. I began to climb up only to be greeted by the polite but firm admonishment of an employee. I was unsure of the words he used but clearly understood that this activity as forbidden as it was foolhardy. I climbed down to the roof and was in the middle of a less than sincere apology when our host smiled and offered to bring wine, cheese and Parma ham to the roof for our delight. He showed us a small table tucked into a corner, and we sat and waited. Shortly thereafter, a small feast of wonderfully sharp cheese, a bottle of smooth Tuscan wine and a plate of tangy Parma ham appeared and we spent the next few hours reclining in our splendor and marveling at our surroundings. We felt like the King and Queen of the castle.

We returned to Rome which now seemed charmingly familiar to us and spent days wandering parks and palaces without a care. Unknown to most casual visitors, there are many places that offer very inexpensive mini-concerts and wonderful music recitals using period instruments in the grand surroundings of twelfth to fifteenth century churches and palaces. A violin recital in the Pamphilli Palace, near the Victor Emmanual monument, and an opera recital in the Church of Agnes in Agone in Piazza Navona, are just two of the many venues we were lucky enough to find. The messages board inside the buildings hold a wealth of information and some surprises, such as announcing a concert on Thursday night, tickets on sale in the gift shop. For ten euros each, we experienced a magical and moving musical evenings.

CHAPTER XXI
Grand Confusione

After spending a month in the Eternal City, we decided to leave Rome for a few days to explore another storied part of this amazing country. The hill towns of Tuscany, to the north of Rome, beckoned like a siren call. However, leaving Rome is not as easy as it sounds. My unfamiliarity with the layout of the city was likely the main issue, but I couldn't help noticing that street names changed every few blocks and construction detours were difficult to navigate with my limited street knowledge. My favorite street sign, after navigating a detour, was still the sign that simply read, "Tutti le Direzione." I now understood that this sign merely pointed the way to a main highway, from which a marginally intelligent driver could then determine which direction to go. After driving for nearly an hour, and coming to the slow realization that I might be one of those marginally intelligent drivers, I was able to locate the main road, the autostrada A-1, very much a modern freeway. We left Rome in the rear view mirror.

About an hour's drive north of Rome there is a place to get gas and refreshment. Ah, but this is no ordinary truck stop. The Auto-Grill stretches across the entire highway and entices drivers in both directions to stop and see what it holds. After parking the car, either stairs or an elevator takes one to the Auto-Grill proper. This is an amazing collection of cafeteria like stalls serving fresh pasta, freshly made grilled panini, roasted meats, an arresting array of freshly sautéed vegetables and more. If that is not enough, there are souvenirs, trinkets, kitchen wares, cups, glasses, mugs, key rings, car fresheners, maps and a full bar. A few small purchases later and after a hearty and unbelievably inexpensive lunch we were about to set out toward our first hilltop destination. But, not before being presented with a "regalo" by the cashier, a ceramic plate emblazoned with flowers, as a "thank you for stopping" gift. It was an unexpected and charming gesture. I still have the plate after these many years.

The hilltop town of Siena is a marvel to explore. After reaching the town and, of course, without any reservations or any thought given to where we would stay, I drove a rather circular road that leads progressively down from the summit of the town. At the second stop which was walking distance to the actual town, I was very pleased to find a well situated hotel room that was perfect for a few days of exploration. I managed to get a room with broken Italian as the mode of conversation. We settled in and headed straight for the center of town on foot. A hot, half hour walk rewarded us with a sight from another time. The present inhabitants of Siena have wisely prohibited cars from using the interior streets. This increases the amount of pedestrian traffic wandering the streets, cafes, shops and ancient sites and gives Siena a feel of conviviality and excitement. One of the main streets holds every designer name imaginable and a few other unfamiliar but as expensive shops. Interspersed between these denizens of haute couture one can find butcher shops, cheese shops, chocolate shops, wine shops and the ever-present souvenir shops. Locals and tourists alike wander the streets. The atmosphere is happy, excited and full of movement. Meandering along with the crowd, the street suddenly opened onto a most magnificent piazza, complete with a fountain, a palace and bell tower.

Piazza del Campo is at the heart of Siena and is its most grand square. Its shape is neither round nor square, more like the shape of a hand held fan with the palace at the bottom and a myriad of restaurants along the top. The imposingly tall red brick bell tower, rising next to the palace, is a perfect square widening with white travertine stone towards the top and crowned with a smaller white travertine tower sprouting from the larger bottom structure. There are four arched windows on each side at an impossible height. On the face of the lower tower is a large clock and just below that, a three story portico style entrance point to the palace. It is a marvel of architecture and beauty. It has been standing here since the 1300s. The Tower of Mangia, we were warned, contains over four hundred stairs on its interior, which leads to what was said to be one of the most magnificent views of the city. It turns out that the stairs are in groups of about eight steps with a turn at every corner landing. Climbing them is an exercise in tight left turns and squeezing past descending bodies. There are very narrow openings through which thankfully refreshing air breathes into the tower. The tower itself is attached to the Palazzo Pubblico, a complex of red brick government buildings that have the appearance of a crenelated castle. These have also been here since the 1300s. The palace contains once magnificent frescos and houses a museum. We overheard a guide, speaking in Italian, explaining that the storage of salt in the basement of the building caused an excessive drying of the frescoed walls leading to their deterioration, a possible but unverifiable story. Still, they are spectacular to view.

A rectangular fountain presents itself in the center toward the rear of the piazza, which is not quite harmonious with the not rectangular piazza. Apparently, the original fountain held a statue of Venus and the pagan nature of the sculpture came to be blamed for the plague that devastated this city in the early 1300s. We were told that the original statue was destroyed and buried outside the city to rid the inhabitants of the evil it represented. The current fountain has breathtaking bas-relief scenes in marble surrounding it on three sides. The water here, we were told, comes from over 15 miles away, quite a feat for a fountain that has been here since at least 1342. The original sculptures were replaced during the 1800s, and I imagine they adorned a private residence before being removed to their current resting place in the Santa Maria Della Scala museum. No matter. The reconstruction is magnificent depicting scenes from ancient Rome, early Christianity, and various figures in exquisite detail. There are wolves at intervals, six in all, around the fountain. Their fierceness somewhat softened by the numerous pigeons sitting on their heads and backs. One is prevented from actually touching the works or the water by a forbidding iron fence that surrounds the entire fountain. This has not stopped tourists from throwing coins into the fountain and certainly provides a secure environment for the multitude of pigeons. I could have spent the day admiring this beautiful and ancient fountain but for the lack of a place to sit and the heat of the noonday sun. Students were happily lounging on the ground in small groups but it seemed wrong to try to join them so we just wandered the piazza seeking refuge and repast at one of the many restaurants ringing the square.

The very next day we again found ourselves moving with the crowd towards the square. Unknown to us, we had arrived in Siena at a most propitious moment. There were people everywhere. The crowds entering this piazza were huge. It was very early in the day and the square was already full. It was difficult to make our way through the crowd who seemed to be mostly locals taken up in some grand celebration. It would be difficult to even find a place to stand, which was what everyone was doing. Everyone was excitedly talking in rapid fire Italian. There was no shortage of good natured insults and laughter all around us. We found a shaded area next to a side building that afforded a somewhat limited view of the piazza. There was a small step here, and if one stepped up, a view of the piazza was possible. Looking back, I am sure I looked like a prairie dog popping up and down trying to view the commotion.

This was the day of the Palio, a famous, twice a year horse race that I had only read about in our guide book. It was our lucky day. The center of the square was cordoned off and the crowd amassed there had very little room to breathe let alone move. But after all, this was the equivalent of the infield at a modern racetrack and was free for the taking. Bleachers and balconies that afforded a much grander view were scarce and expensive. I had never seen such a crowd. A course had been laid out around the piazza, and the stone flooring was covered with a thick layer of clay and sand watered down to create a somewhat stable race track. At one end, a heavy rope was suspended across the course as the official starting line. The anticipation was palpable.

Siena is composed of several ancient villages that came together to form this city. The individual identities of the now seventeen various neighborhoods, called Contrade, is not lost on the current residents, and each identifies strongly with his or her own neighborhood. Rivalries are strong and pride overflows during the Palio. Each separate neighborhood of Siena has a horse and a rider that compete in this race for the honor of winning a banner depicting the Virgin Mary, the Palio. This race has been held since the 1600s and is at once festive and competitive. Ten out of the seventeen neighborhoods compete in each race in a grand, twice a year spectacle that is difficult to understand for the outsider. I heard tales of riders and horses being poisoned, beaten, kidnapped and worse in the days before a race. The horses are hidden from view in the week leading up to the race. The riders secluded from their rivals. Money changes hands, bribes are handed out, bets are placed, there are whispers of nefarious deeds and a fierce rivalry is apparent.

There are eleven streets that lead into the square. Half of these were nearly blocked by long tables at which the inhabitants of that contrade sat, ate, drank and discussed the event to come. This was not a time for the casual tourist, and we were roundly ignored as we had made our way through this throng. A parade begins the festivities. From the remaining streets came the costumed and colorful parade participants. A roar from the crowd greeted each group as they entered the square. Each neighborhood has its own crest. These are placed on colorful flags held on long poles and ceremoniously thrown aloft and deftly caught by the bearer. I never saw one hit the ground. This is a practiced skill and no doubt, a fallen flag would mean disgrace to the flag bearer. Each bearer is brightly costumed and marches in formation with his fellow brethren, flags spinning and flying proudly.

At long last several horses and riders appeared and began to line up at the rope barrier. There were ten in all. There are no saddles. This is a bareback event harking back to a more primitive time. Riders are young men dressed in the finest silk and satin, emblazoned with their district colors. You are at once transported back to medieval times. The horses are adorned with flowing blankets of blue, gold and red. A hush descends over the crowd as the riders jockey for position along the rope. The horses seem to sense the importance of the coming race, and the riders have a very difficult time containing them. All the while, an announcer can be heard over a loudspeaker speaking the words that all can agree upon, "Grand Confusione! Grand Confusione!" Horses and riders pushed past the rope, backing and turning seemingly at will. Finally, after the third announcement of "Grand Confusione" the rope was dropped and the horses and riders sprinted away.

At the very first turn, the third horse lost it's footing. Clay and sand went flying as horse and rider crashed to the ground. The rider slammed against the Palace wall and lay still on the ground, while the now rider-less horse arose and rejoined the race, still not in last place. This race is three laps and takes less than two minutes to complete. Horses are pushed past the point of safety into the turns. Riders do not yield the field and horses and riders bump and scrape each other as they fly past. One horse and rider became tangled up with the fallen rider and fell behind by three lengths. The rider urging his horse with all his soul to catch the others. In the final lap, on the second to the last turn, the lead horse, whose rider apparently did not study the physics of motion and friction, entered the turn much too fast, and the horse slid with all four feet sideways across the course taking out three others as it fell. The rest of the field came barreling into the turn, now littered with fallen horses and riders and promptly stumbled and fell creating a heap of writhing animal and human bodies. The last horse and rider, who had been unable to catch the pack until now, angled his horse to the outside of the track, almost scraping the building but moving past the pile of unseated riders and horses. In this way he managed to become the front runner, indeed, the only runner, and crossed the finish line in triumph.

Pandemonium broke out. Thousands joined the infield. Barriers were broken and overrun. The rider was taken from his horse by the crowd. He laid across the crowd with arms extended Christ-like on his back and was passed hand to hand until he reached his own rejoicing district. There he was lofted into the air while tears of joy streamed from his face and from the faces of all those around him. This group surged toward the cathedral for the awarding of the Palio to the victorious contrade.

Try as we did, there was no way to reach the cathedral in this crowd. All were pushing, crying, arguing, laughing, and singing caught up in the mass hysteria that followed this race. We felt lucky to have seen the spectacle and lucky to have escaped the crowd as we walked back down the road to the relative quiet of our hotel.

CHAPTER XXII
Living In A Postcard

The decision to continue our northward trek and visit Lake Como was an easy one to make. Virtually every guide book and every account by past visitors we knew spoke of picture perfect villages, dramatic Alpine views, a laid back cafe lifestyle, and famous villas and gardens to behold. I made our reservation through a third party for the magnificently pictured Grand Hotel Imperiale. It was directly on the lake. We would be their guest for four glorious nights.

Setting out the next morning very early, I determined the we would have plenty of time to visit the famous Milan Cathedral before heading to Como. After all, this was said to be one of the largest and oldest cathedrals in Italy and had apparently taken six centuries to complete. That was something not to be missed, and it was on our way according to the paper map in my possession in these pre-GPS days. A word about GPS technology. While this invention is surely the best navigational tool ever, it does take the mystery and wonder out of the experience of driving in a new and unknown countryside. Getting lost and having to find one's way, interacting with locals for directions and discovering places you never intended to discover is an experience I fear will be lost to the next generation. Alexa, Siri, Cortona and Google simply cannot replace the absolute enjoyment of self-navigating back roads, having to back out of too narrow streets and finally finding your way when you thought all was lost. These experiences are the stories you will remember most and retell to your friends over many a glass of wine and with much laughter. Besides, one cannot fully trust a GPS that has no sense of danger as it blithely tells you to turn left on a mountain road that would send you crashing down to highway below when the road no longer exists. But I digress.

In Milan, Piazza del Duomo, in the center of the city, is a large pedestrian square directly in front of the cathedral. It is lined on both sides by colonnaded arcades, arched walkways and magnificent buildings. To the left of the cathedral is the Galleria Vittorio Emanuele II, an arched glass and steel arcade that beckons one to enter what is perhaps the most beautiful indoor shopping mall ever created. Beautiful glass covered archways lead to a massive glass and steel dome that covers the central area and captivates your view. This magnificent passageway leads to the Teatro alla Scala, the famous opera house whose architecture, while grand, pales in comparison. There are no bargains in these shops, but the view and awe-inspiring sense of grandeur is well worth the walk.

The gothic cathedral towers over the square and is indeed massive. The height of the structure is a dizzying 350 feet, and the ornamentation appears lavishly overdone as was the style of the day. Some 3,000 plus statues adorn the cathedral. There are literally over a thousand spires reaching skyward. Flying buttresses are all topped with ornate lattice-like stone walls and additional spires. It takes a while to let this grandiose edifice settle into your consciousness. As with many constructions of this era, one is left wondering how these ancient people accomplished this task without electricity, motorized power or modern cranes. The fact that this church has lasted hundreds of years speaks to the ingenuity and skill of the architects, builders and craftsman who toiled for many long years. It is humbling to think that a person who began working on this structure could work their entire life and never see the completed project. That vision would wait for several generations beyond one short lifetime.

The lines to enter the cathedral were exceedingly long and we determined that we should visit another day on our return from Lago di Como. We hastened back to the car and set out in the direction where I had imagined that the lake was waiting for us.

Let me explain something about Italian traffic signs in crowded Italian cities. For one not familiar with the streets,

straight to the right, which I followed by turning right. A looping road placed me back on the bridge in the opposite direction. At the other end of the bridge I encountered a sign that pointed out Lago di Como to the direct left and I made the left turn. After a few minutes of driving in this direction, another sign pointed upwards and left, except there were two streets to the left. I took the larger of two possible leftward streets. Another short while found a sign pointing again to the right, and turning right, I found myself back of the very same bridge headed toward Milan and away from Lago di Como. The laughter erupting from my darling passenger only added to the charm of the moment, and her constant helpful suggestion that I ask someone for directions only made my resolve all the more firm. However, the third time I was crossing the bridge, I pulled over into a gas station, not intending to ask directions, but to buy a better map. As I looked through the maps available, a kindly young man, probably a student from the youthful looks of him seemed to take pity on me and asked in Italian where I was going. I answered, also in Italian, that I was completely lost and trying to find Lago di Como. He smiled broadly at my poor use of the language and asked, in English, if I would mind if he spoke English to me as he needed the practice. I quickly agreed. After beginning to explain the route, he stopped mid-sentence and said, "Just follow me." He hopped in his car and I followed as I was told. Within five minutes he signaled me to turn onto the freeway where a sign said Lago di Como with an arrow pointing straight up. I waved in thanks and headed down the road. By the way, if you miss the turnoff to Lago di Como from this freeway, you will be in Switzerland. I did not make that mistake and Lago di Como magically appeared ahead of us.

The hotel I had chosen turned out not to be in Como at all. It was definitely on the lake but in Tremezzo, a small town just north of Como on the West side of the lake. From here, one has a magical view of Bellagio directly across the lake on the opposite shore. The Hotel Imperiale is a grand hotel just across the highway from the lakeside docks. Its facade rises against a lush green hillside that frames the hotel like a 3D photograph. A dozen clear story windows crown its roof line and in front there is a grand apartment with a charming raised terrace straight out of a Roman villa with colonnaded walls and a striking view of the lake itself. I congratulated myself on my choice of lodgings. The feeling of accomplishment was not lasting.

At the reception, I proudly announced in Italian that I had a reservation for four nights. The extremely well dressed clerk dutifully checked his register, frowned and looked at me over his glasses with a polite but somewhat condescending glance. "I am very sorry, sir, but you do not appear to be listed as a guest here. Are you sure you have the right hotel?" This response was, I am quite sure, at least partially due to the disheveled appearance I must have presented after driving for hours and for wearing worn jeans in such a fine establishment. I summoned my most patrician voice and assured him I was in the right place. After a frantic few minutes, I presented him with whatever documentation I could find amongst my various papers. He looked them over and went to the phone to make a call. After what sounded like some polite but firm exchange, he returned and explained that the company I used for this booking had not sent the telex of my reservation and so there was no record of the booking at the hotel. This was followed by an apologetic, "At the moment we have no rooms available in the main hotel." At that moment, the telex began its chore of churning out our pre-paid reservation. The clerk looked at it with concern and returned to the counter with a magnanimous air. "I do have a room you can use for the night, after which I will transfer you to the room you have reserved." I was so happy that I would not have to go in search of another hotel and brave the hassle of trying to get a refund that I think I audibly sighed with relief. The ring of the desk bell summoned the bellman for our bags, and we were escorted out of the lobby towards the free-standing villa in the front park-like grounds of the hotel.

At first, I thought we were going to an outbuilding nearby that looked more like an ornate garden shed than a hotel room. It turned out to be just that and we continued toward the main building. Thankfully, we would not be staying there. I reminded myself that the hotel was making a gracious gesture for which I should have been showing more gratitude. The bellman then deftly strode up the steps of the grand villa and opened the door, stepping aside for my wife to pass into a palatial room. The marble floors and gilded furniture were enough to take your breath away. Fine art prints and oil paintings adorned the walls. A quick tour took us through a sitting room, a living room, a kitchen, an enormous bedroom, two bathrooms, a sun room and then onto a large exterior terrace from which there was an unobstructed view of the lake. I was quite overwhelmed while my wife acted as if this was to be expected and as it should be. I thanked the bellman, tipped him generously and turned to my wife. Holding out my hand and somewhat incongruously humming the Waltz of the Blue Danube, I danced my wife around the terrace with great sweeping strides. We stopped to look out at the lake and to wave, in a royal fashion of course, to passersby. I did my best to imitate a truly upper-class wave, hand raised to the level of my eyebrow, hand facing toward me and executing two quick outward movements, like tipping a hat except there was no hat. I am sure the people below were no doubt wondering who this grand couple might be, or at least that is the way I choose to recall it.

CHAPTER XXIII
Venice and the Aqua Alta

When planning to visit Venice, one's main concern becomes trying to avoid a time when the city will be so flooded with tourists from cruise ships and day trippers that site seeing becomes an impossible chore. I had seen pictures of wall to wall tourists on narrow canal bridges all jostling for a perfect selfie and was determined to miss that experience. We chose a time when we hoped the city would be less crowded and other Americans would be home celebrating Halloween and Thanksgiving. As far as the crowds were concerned, this was perfect timing.

Our train deposited us at the Venice station where we joined others trying to get a boat to our specific hotel. Hardly unique, I had chosen a hotel promising a view of a picturesque canal. Transportation from the train station is by a multi passenger boats called a vaporetti, which are quite inexpensive, or by a smaller private taxi boat, which are not so inexpensive. The vaporetti make regular stops at predetermined locations which are numbered for convenience. Before boarding, we were directed to a book with hotel names and a corresponding vaporetti stops by number. One boards the vaporetto, bags in tow, and waits until the boat stops at the announced stop. We were at stop number four. As we exited the vaporetto we were approached by a porter who offered to bring us and our bags to the hotel in question. Hotel Moises was over three bridges and down a long canal. I am not sure I would have found it without assistance. I was very grateful for this friendly service.

Once at the hotel, we climbed two flights of narrow stairs to find our room down an equally narrow hall. The walls were adorned with velvet wall paper in opulent reds and greens with gold accents. The room had a small window that opened outward onto a canal below. There was a landing where a fruit laden barge was off loading its cargo for the open market. We marveled at how this system operated, and has probably operated, for over a thousand years. The boatsman was strong and his seaworthy legs never faltered as he transitioned from water to land carrying boxes of every fruit imaginable. Later, we would watch again as the empty boxes and refuse was loaded on yet another barge to be disposed of, we know not where.

I considered us lucky to be near a central point where gondola rides were offered to tourists. This point of reference was an invaluable guide in the maze of canals, bridges, walkways and piazzas that is Venice. I learned that by walking through St. Mark's Square to the far left corner would lead to a passageway that wound its way to my reference point. From there, the hotel was a short walk across one bridge. Nearly everyone, even fellow tourists, could point out the direction of St. Mark's Square and so getting lost was minimized.

On this day the weather was threatening rain but the sun was fighting a valiant battle to overcome the gloom. We set out towards the military shipyards on the side of the island opposite St. Mark's Square. Following a canal and crossing several bridges brought us to an arched gateway. On the other side was the sea with a walkway along the sea wall. It was made of wood and seemed to stretch for a long distance around this part of Venice. We began walking and admiring the view and the few boats we saw in the distance. Somehow, the walkway turned into a ledge along the sea wall. We were on the water side of the wall with no entrance back to the city. When faced with a choice of continuing into uncertainty or turning back, I of course opted for the uncertainty. As we continued, the sun began to lose its battle to the forces of the rain gods. Large drops began to fall, a few at first and then suddenly a deluge. Just by chance, I spied another arched gateway and we ran toward it for shelter. As we stood under the arch, the sky opened in earnest and the rain was so thick that it was difficult to see beyond a few feet. Still, we could hear the voices of children screeching and laughing in the distance. As the rain lessened, we ventured out and headed toward the voices. Thankfully, the children had just come from school and were headed en masse to a vaporetto to go home. We followed them and boarded the vaporetto which was now filled with drenched children and two very out of place adults. The six euro fare was not collected as everyone was trying to find a dry spot to stand or sit and chaos prevailed. This was the longest vaporetto trip we have ever taken. The boat went around the entire back side of the island finally coming to one of two stops at St. Mark's Square. I lead the way off at the first stop, the wrong one, and we walked back in a light rain to the main square. From there, my reference point did not fail me, and we arrived back at the hotel wet but relieved.

After drying off, I pushed open the window to behold a magnificent afternoon sunshine drenching the canal and creating a magical view of shimmering beauty. The gondolas for hire had begun again, and we gazed at the passing tourists as we dried our hair with our towels. Friendly waves from strangers left a feeling of warmth and welcome even if we would never actually meet them. The sounds of Italian songs, accordion music and chatter reached our ears, and we felt at one with the city.

As November came upon us, we were witness to a yearly phenomena called Aqua Alta, the high water. We were unaware that this was a normal part of the Venetian experience if you happened to be here during the fall. At first we wondered why all the merchants in St. Mark's Square were moving merchandise from their lower shelves. Why were the municipal authorities setting up large wooden planks across triangular metal stands two feet high? These temporary structures soon encircled the entirety of St. Mark's square, and none too soon. It seems that at this time of year, the drains through which water normally passes out to the sea, reverse themselves as the level of the lagoon rises, and the water comes into the city through the drains filling the squares and indeed most of the city with water. What begins as a series of puddles soon escalates into a shallow lake and them becomes a city lagoon. This particular year, the water reached such a height that the wooden planks, set up to provide a walkway for the occasion, simply floated away. Tourists waded across the square holding bags aloft as they made their way to and from the hotels and the vaporetti. St. Marks was under three feet of water and only tall or foolish people ventured out. When it was our turn to go, we were grateful for the gondola stop nearby the hotel restaurant. Normally bringing the well heeled to the canal side restaurant, we found that for a small fortune we could go from the restaurant landing to a waiting vaporetto. In this way we were able to escape the fate of the tourist we saw slip while lofting his bag overhead and gently slide into the waters of the newly created interior lagoon that was formerly St. Marks Square.

The engineers of Italy and indeed the entire European world have been hard at work on a novel solution to this annual issue. I heard they have placed great iron plates on the bottom of the lagoon which theoretically can be raised to keep out the water as it rises in the lagoon thereby saving the city from the annual flood. So far, this is just a theory although I understand millions of euros have been poured into the project. I am guessing that the people of Venice, who have lived with Aqua Alta for centuries, are merely amused that mortals think they can alter nature in this way. The Venetians will likely continue their lives as they have always done in spite of these well meaning efforts. Lower floors are abandoned to the eroding effects of the water, and residents have simply moved to higher floors. Aqua Alta also seems to provide the canals with an infusion of cleansing sea water, and the lack of this natural flushing out effect will likely be another new problem to take on if the grand lagoon plates experiment succeeds. Time will tell.

It seemed a good time to leave Venice behind and head south to warmer and less wet climes. We drove for hours, stopped in small towns for lunch and coffee, amused the locals in a truck stop that never saw tourists passing through and struggled with unattended gas stations that seemed not to want to take my Euros. Kindly drivers helped me to operate the pumps, and we were again on our southbound journey.

CHAPTER XXIV
Greek Temples and Funny Money

Just below Naples is the port city of Salerno and just to the south of Salerno is rumored to be the best preserved Greek temples in all of Italy. With a paper map to guide us and my wife as our trusty navigator, we set out from Naples and began our southward voyage into the unknown. Our destination was the city of Paestum, where we had heard were reconstructed Greek temples complete with all their columns now intact and the facade an unrivaled sight to behold.

I had navigated into Naples in the middle of the night by following signs that read "Centro" with what looked like a bullseye next to it. I had stopped a gendarme at the side of the road, well past midnight, to get reoriented after several "centro" sighs seemed to lead in circles. He was kind and forgiving of my fractured use of his beautiful language and pointed us in the right direction. Turning downhill inevitably led to the water where we found Hotel Miramar waiting for us just across from the grand Castel dell'Ovo set in the middle of the bay.

Getting out of Naples was not so easy. I drove in the direction of what I imagined was the main highway only to find myself staring again at the sea of Naples from a slightly different angle. My navigator's insistent question—What street is this?— seemed unhelpful at that moment. At last, a "tutti le dirrecione" sign appeared mercifully pointing the way to everywhere. We took the direction toward Salerno and were soon following the well-marked signs to our new destination, Paestum.

Turning off the main highway and following a westward road soon brought us to a very small town with very few lodgings. Of course, my lack of planning was not actually helpful, and we finally found ourselves at a seaside, two story house that offered rooms to let. The proprietress seemed rather severe, and as she handed over the keys, made sure I understood that after 11:00 pm the doors would be locked and not opened again until morning. Our key was to our room, not to the house. I nodded and did my best to look dutifully impressed as I pocketed the key. It was getting late and the wonderful smells coming from a nearby restaurant/pizzeria compelled us to follow the scent of garlic, herbs and tomatoes to the entrance of what turned out to be a very quaint restaurant. We were shown a seat by the window with a view of the sea. I inquired in Italian if they accepted traveler's checks and was met with a crisp "Certo!" Thankfully, traveler's checks are now a completely unnecessary and burdensome way to bring money into another country. With the ready availability of credit cards and ATMs, there is really no reason to bring hundreds of dollars in pretty blue checks with the American Eagle on them, sign and counter sign and show a passport to use this substitute for real money. However, on this trip some well meaning friends had convinced me that a traveler's check was worth the trouble and could never be used by others if lost, and I succumbed to the thought of monetary security without thinking it through.

We dined that night on a delicious pizza with a simple salad and even had room for dessert. Finally, after ordering espresso, I requested the bill. It was delivered immediately with a smile. The total was $42.00 after converting from local currency. I took out a one hundred-dollar traveler's check, showed it to the waiter, had him watch while I countersigned it, took out my passport and wrote the number on the check which the waiter verified was correct. I then took out a small calculator and did the math while slowly enunciating each number clearly as I punched the buttons on the calculator. When finished, I showed the waiter the total amount that he owed me, which was of course more that the cost of the dinner, $58.00. He nodded in assent and said "Subito!" and took the bill and the check to the back of the restaurant.

My wife and I enjoyed the leisurely coffee and after a long while began thinking about the possibility of being locked out of our accommodations. I scanned the restaurant for our waiter and found him surrounded by five other people all very interested in whatever he was holding in his hand. After a moment, I realized that my traveler's check was the center of all this attention. I watched as the check was lifted up to the light, turned front to back and upside down, and then passed around the circle of concern that had developed. An older gentleman, whom I took to be the owner, grabbed the check and headed for the phone. After some excited conversation and several exasperated gestures, he returned, and the circle of concern formed again. Once again the check was passed from hand to hand, each person adding their commentary, shaking their heads and turning their palms up to the sky. The whole procession moved into the kitchen out of my sight, and I imagined the chef would now carve up the check to see if there was money inside. In due time, the group reappeared, and another phone call was placed. This one ended with a bang of the receiver. Soon after, our waiter appeared table side, as professional as one could be, smiled broadly and placed a silver tray with $58.00 in local currency in front of me. No other words were spoken. I left a generous tip even though I knew that service was included. Our waiter was pleased, and I was sure the owner would be at the bank the next morning hoping he had made the correct choice.

We strolled back to find our front door locked. We were fifteen minutes early, how could this be? I knocked loudly and our stern but diminutive host appeared somewhat perturbed with a bundle of keys. I pointed to my watch, and she grudgingly opened the door. We scampered up the stairs and were grateful to be home at last.

The following morning, we went out to see the three Greek temples we had read about. I was surprised to learn that almost 50% of the town is private land and has not been excavated. What mysteries must still exist under the houses, businesses and large open fields of this area? One can see that the ancient defensive city walls still exist and are broken only by a modern highway that neatly bisects the area. The walls look about six feet thick and about 30 feet high. There are towers at intervals much higher than this. From what I could see, the construction looked like very large stones of various sizes all stacked one upon the other with just their sheer weight holding them together. A variety of grasses and weeds protruded from the cracks. Nature knows no bounds.

Greek temples are marvelous structures even when surrounded by dry grasses and a forbidding fence. There were no guards, and on this day, the enormous site seemed to be abandoned. No tourist groups or buses were in sight. Our guide book seemed a little confusing. This city it seems was not Paestum but the Doric Greek city of Poseidonia, named after the Greek god of the Sea. It would not be Paestum for another three hundred plus years after its founding. There were two Temples of Hera and one of Athena. One of the Temples of Hera, the second one, was also the Temple of Neptune. The first Temple of Hera was also a temple of Zeus. I had trouble figuring out which was which. Next time I will get a better book.

The fence around each temple was a low structure made of wood cross beams that gave the impression of an American Western corral that surrounded each one. The first Temple of Hera, said to be the oldest, is dated from about 550BC although this date is in some dispute as various other sources have differing dates, and there doesn't seem to be anyone left who actually knows when the first stone was laid. The columns are massive and hold up equally massive stones for the roof supports. Alas, the roofs are long gone. I am constantly amazed that the ancients could accomplish such massive building feats without modern equipment. The fluted columns at their widest point seem to be about eight feet in diameter. Their weight must be enormous. The temple is a rectangular structure with nine columns in the front and eighteen columns along each side. A slow circumnavigation takes at least 20 minutes. The low fence seemed almost an invitation to trespass, which I did briefly before my sense of right and wrong finally stopped me. I did briefly scamper into the temple, take a very quick look around and hustled out before any invisible guards could sternly rebuke me. Millions of people had come here in ancient times to worship, I figured that neither Hera, Zeus, Poseidon, Athena nor Neptune would have minded my brief visit even if the current authorities might have a different view. The late afternoon sun seemed to light the temple from within, and it glowed a warm brownish-reddish hue in its solitude.

The second Temple of Hera, according to the book, is also the one called the Temple of Neptune and is said to date from 450BC. It is a smaller structure with just six columns in front and fourteen columns along the sides. There are three huge steps leading up to the temple on all sides. The ancient Greeks must have struggled to enter this place as I did to get a picture. The facade of the front entrance is wonderfully preserved and is indeed massive. At first glance it resembles a building that is perched atop the columns. The upper structure, to which the roof would have been attached, is a triangular masterpiece that defies the ages. That it has survived intact is a wonder.

Set apart from these two, the Temple of Athena looks more ancient than its neighbors. Our book says 500BC but who knows. These sites were erected, abandoned, partially destroyed by Vesuvius, occupied by invaders, again neglected, rediscovered and finally made UNESCO Heritage sites in 1998. The Temple of Athena has six columns in front and 13 along the sides. It is apart from the others and tucked into some trees which makes it picturesque and also wonderfully shaded for those like myself wanting to rest out of the noonday sun. Why the Temple of Athena is apart from the others remains a mystery to me. The other two temples are directly next to each other as if there was some ancient competition to build it bigger and better. Stately Athena sits on a little higher ground and seems above the fray.

There are other structures here, including a Greek tomb that was discovered as late as 1952. It lies in the middle of the settlement surrounded by a thick wall. Its triangular roof structure juts above the ground and looks to be made of ten large clay tiles on each side of the pointed roof. What lies below is anyone's guess as I could not locate an above ground entrance. I wondered how deep into the ground this structure was embedded. It resembled a small house that had been swallowed by a rising land mass, leaving only the roof to breathe in the remaining air. There is also a small amphitheater consisting of about eight levels of seats surrounding a thirty-foot diameter circular area seemingly suited to discussions rather than spectacles. Sitting on these steps brings a sense of history and awe. Others sat here over 2000 years ago. It left me speechless.

CHAPTER XXV
Cinque Terre

On the Ligurian Coast there are five villages that have taken on a storied life in the annals of tourism. Cinque Terre is a collection of four small seaside towns and one hilltop town that cooperate to produce wines from unbelievably steeply terraced vineyards. The towns are linked with a train that stops at each one and boats ply the waters between the towns bringing mostly tourists and a few locals from one town to another. For the more athletically inclined, there is a path leading from each village that goes up the mountain, across to the next hill and down into the next town. This series of paths, which take anywhere from twenty minutes to one hour each were free for the walking until recently. The deluge of tourists following the guide book driven popularity of this area have degraded the paths, crowded the towns and finally led to the imposition of a fee for each leg of the journey. Recent mudslides have also destroyed a portion of the path which required rebuilding. It seems that an inordinate number of people want to walk all five of the towns in a single day. To do so is a great disservice to the area and does not allow one to experience the life of the villages beyond getting a gelato and lunch.

My wife and I decided to stay in Monterosso al Mare as our base of operations. This is the largest and most urbanized of the towns. It consequently has the most accommodations and restaurants. The beach has rentable cabanas and chairs. There is a hotel at the top of a bluff called Porto Della Rocca where we found a beautiful accommodation. From our balcony, we could see a portion of the coast, watch fishermen and their boats in the morning and bask in the light of the sunsets. Monterosso has a narrow and crowded beach with a clock tower overlooking the scene. The houses are yellows, ochres and warm browns that are set in a backdrop of impossibly green hills. Some of the terraced vineyards can be seen from the beach.

The town itself seems evenly divided between the old and the new. There is a tunnel that leads from one section to another, and while there were many fellow tourists walking from section to section, there were also cars and small trucks that occasionally plied this road making the walk seem a little less ideal. The old town contains the Church of St. John the Baptist said to date from the late 1200s. There is a famous convent with notable art works that attracts most tourists for a brief visit. Staying in Monterosso al Mare allows one to become immersed in the village rhythm of life, tasty focaccia in the morning while sitting on a sea wall, espresso while standing at a bar, strolling through the village both old and new, dining in the new town at

devour the panini we had brought with us, drink some Cinque Terre wine and give ourselves over to peaceful contemplation. This reverie was promptly broken by at least a dozen children apparently let loose from their confines who tagged and screamed their way past us with wild laughter. Looking back in the direction from whence they came brought the one of the sad realities of Italy back to the forefront. The children had a picnic of their own, leaving behind all of the detritus one would expect, candy wrappers, soda cans, and paper bags. There was no trashcan in sight, and the responsible hiker's motto "pack it in, pack it out" was unknown here. Our thoughts thus interrupted, we decided to follow the path in the direction of the next town that was not a part of the Cinque Terre experience, Levanto.

The path from the ruins of the church to Levanto is a wide, easy to walk pine needle covered experience. On the left are absolutely beautiful views of the sea sandwiched between the trees. There is no precipitous cliff like drop offs to deal with and no groups of backpackers crowding the path. The air is pine scented, the sky blue and the sounds are nature's own chorus of birds, wind and rustling leaves. Just as the trail begins its downward slope into the town below, there is a small cafe with a wonderful view seemingly in the middle of nowhere. We stopped here to order a glass of wine, sit and enjoy our surroundings. It was a perfect spot, and we lingered for an hour before deciding that we needed to move on if we were to see any part of Levanto and make our way back before dark.

We descended into the town and were immediately met with an historic and well preserved thirteenth century loggia. I know this because there was a very useful sign pointing this out. I stepped beyond the iron fencing and stood where I imagined countless members of Roman royal families had stood over the ages. This loggia is at ground level with columns and pillars. One side faces a large piazza aptly named Piazza della Loggia. There was a castle I wanted to visit, but as we engaged in brief conversation with the proprietor of a cafe, we learned that it was closed to the public. In any event, the sun was now getting low in the sky and we decided that we should begin our walk back to Monterosso al Mare before the darkness made the path too dark to travel. The return trip was just as magical as the way there as we were again fully engulfed in the scents of pine and olives. Climbing down the giant's steps was easier than going up, and we soon found ourselves at our basecamp. I had been eyeing a restaurant near the beach, and we decided that is where we would dine tonight. It did not disappoint with professionally proud Italian service and fine seafood that tasted as if it were caught that morning. Thinking back, I am sure it was.

CHAPTER XXVI
Vernazza and More

The most picturesque town of the five villages is un-doubtably the fishing village of Vernazza. Its central street is framed by buildings rising on both sides with narrow stairs and walkways leading to dead end passages and a maze of narrow alleys between the tall buildings. One can easily lose oneself here while exploring the town. Not to worry though as every downhill path leads back to the main street bisecting the town. This street is lined with seafood restaurants and cafes that all beckon to the passing tourist. There is a small angular seawall protecting the town and providing yet another popular prome-nade and picture taking spot. Fishing boats, small, wooden and colorful, line the small harbor and seawall.

Getting to Vernazza is accomplished in one of four ways. The least used is the ribbon of a road atop the mountain which connects each of the towns, and in the case of Vernazza, leads to a parking area high above the actual town. One can park here for a fee and walk down into the town. There are no cars allowed in the main town and really no need for them. The main street is steep and charming with all manner of shops, grocers, tourist trinkets and restaurants.

The second way is the train system, also connecting the towns. Each successive town is a mere ten-minute train ride from the other. The towns can also be inadvertently missed this way if one boards the wrong train, as it turns out that some trains stop at each town while others skip from first to last. I know this because one unfortunate afternoon I relied on my excellent ability to speak Italian with the station master and bought a ticket for the wrong train. We were promptly deposited two towns past our destination. I suppose I should be grateful that we didn't end up many more miles away.

The third way in to Vernazza is the most frequented. It is of course the trail system linking the towns. One begins at the beach, hiking up into the terraced vineyards on the hills, crossing the mountainside on trails sometimes so narrow as not to allow two persons to pass, carefully navigating the path leading between a sheer drop into the sea and the wall of a vineyard terrace and eventually hiking downhill into the town below. At every step there are views demanding to be photographed. The vista is astonishing. A mere hour and a half from Monterosso al Mare finds one enjoying a coffee in Vernazza. We passed an inordinate number of German tourists on the day we chose for our hike. The language is not the only give away. Hiking in shorts, carrying duel rubber tipped aluminum walking sticks and burdened with backpacks, these sturdy and determined individuals seem to come in droves, one after the other, and sometimes side by side, making the walk perilous indeed. We met one such young woman who was covered in scratches, fresh with blood. Our brief inquiry made us understand that when the trail narrows ahead there was no room for passing with a backpack causing her to be bumped off the trail by her companion and into thick thorn covered bramble on the side of the cliff. If not for getting her backpack struck on the thorns, she would have plunged a long way to the rocky coast below. We waited until we could see a break in the steady stream of hikers and made our way beyond the thin strip of pathway while clinging to the side of the mountain for safety. Terrible rain storms here have washed out parts of this trail in the years since we visited. Vernazza all but disappeared under more than ten feet of mud and debris that churned down the steep hillsides. Even the train station was not spared and became buried in mud further isolating the town. These resilient people were undeterred, and the town again sparkles with life. The trails have been reconstructed and since passage is now paid for by each traveler, I suspect the trail is wider and easier to walk than before.

The final and easiest way to enter Vernazza is by boat. There is a popular ferry between the towns full of bathing suited tourists. The boats are small, locally run and seem to be frequent. One can visit four out of five towns this way. The town of Cornelia is located above the sea at the top of a mountain path, inaccessible by boat and so the least crowded.

Once in Vernazza, the feeling of being caught up in a fairy tale is inescapable. The town is bathed in light coming from the sea illuminating the rust, orange, yellow, green, and pink buildings on both sides of the main road. At the foot of the main road is a courtyard of sorts with brightly colored umbrellas crowded with tables from both restaurants and gelaterias. The beach is no more than a fifty-yard spit of sand, covered equally with colorful wooden fishing boats pulled out of the small harbor, and a few determined tourists trying to catch the sun. A walkway continues along the southernmost buildings and leads out to the jetty which blocks the sea from overwhelming the town, at least when there are no storms to contend with. One side of the jetty is concrete and easy to walk while the other is quite rough with large rocks that lead out into the sea. Just to the left is what appears to be an ancient square tower three stories high with an incline ramp leading from the jetty to the first level of the tower. Stairs then take over the job of transporting people upward to the second level and finally to the roof where there is a stunningly perched restaurant with magnificent views and cool breezes. This turns out to be the perfect place to relax with a cocktail of your choice and thoughts of high seas piracy, at least in the purely romantic version that plays in my head. The fact that these towns were besieged by real pirates in the past only heightens the imagination of the land lubbers that come here to dream.

On a promontory set apart from the town is a round tower called the Belfort Tower. It was most likely built by the Genovese in perhaps the twelfth or thirteenth century to afford the town residents a view of nearly the entire coastline. The better to see the pirates as they approached. Around the tower is a fortress, Doria Castle, that undoubtedly was used in the defense of the town. We were made to understand that this castle was used again by the Nazis in WWII and subsequently bombed by the allies. It was rebuilt and stands as a proud monument to the town's storied past. This extraordinary tower can be viewed close up by paying a small fee or from a short distance on the path leading either to or away from the town to the south, depending on which way you are headed. In either case, it is a powerful example of the trials and tribulations that faced these hearty people.

Back in Monterosso we discovered a most wonderful after dinner wine not available anywhere outside these villages. Schachettra is a golden colored, late harvest wine produced from the grapes left on the vines until they are nearly raisins. These are picked and hand selected for the nectar that can be squeezed and fermented into a striking sweet wine. Having en-

countered this wine and its explanation in a local wine shop, I
was determined to buy some and transport it back to the States.

      The wine shop in the old part of the town was located
by following the sounds of Mozart that was wafting through the
street. Fully expecting to find a music store, we stumbled upon a
cave-like structure with candle lit wine barrels for tables and the
most beautiful music emanating from its interior. As we entered
we were met by the proprietor, a jovial if thoughtful man who
spoke perfect English with a delicious Italian accent. He waved
us to a table and we enjoyed a few glasses of wines we had never heard of but nonetheless found very appealing. As we were
about to leave, we asked if he had the storied wine of Cinque
Terre, Schacciatra. His eyes lit up and he proceeded to explain
the painstaking method of this wine's preparation, which we
knew but enjoyed hearing again. Of course, we had to try a
glass before departing. Now, I must tell you, I am not usually a
fan of dessert wines. I find them to be cloyingly sweet and
overpriced. But this wine, well, it was sublime. The sweetness
was more subtle and the flavor of the grape was more pro-
nounced. Its color was that of a golden goblet. One glass, and I
was hooked. He explained several different vintages to us showing prices that went from modestly expensive to very expensive.
I explained that we were here for a few more days, and we
would come back to purchase a few bottles on the day we were

leaving. We visited this magical, cozy wine bar twice more that week, but the day of our departure brought a different experience and resulted in a purchase from his competitor just a short walk away.

After enjoying a morning slice of onion and olive focaccia by the Monterosso al Mare seawall, I noticed a small, local wine shop just a few steps up the road. It held no pretense and was run by a capable young woman who seemed happy that we had ventured into her shop. A moment later I was looking at the same vintages and bottles of the magic elixir at less than half the price. I made my purchases and left feeling that I had stumbled upon a bit of good luck. I bought an extra bottle that I was sure would not make it back to the States, its allure compelling us to sample it again and again before the long airplane ride home.

FINAL THOUGHTS
Magical Moments

Italy, for my wife and I, will always hold a certain fascination and love that is not easily defined. The ancient sights unique to each town and city are certainly places to be seen and experienced, but it is the people and the feeling that this country in particular allows one to indulge in a free spirited outlook that bring us back again and again. There are so many small, picturesque towns to see and so many kind, quirky and wonderful people to meet, one could spend a lifetime here and still have more to discover. We shall without a doubt return as often as we can.

And I must tell you, that no matter where I find myself, not a day that goes by that the smell of fish still provokes the strongest memories of a Sicilian adventure, and I find myself right back in Palermo standing on a balcony overlooking a fish market and hearing the calls of the vendors in sing-song melody...."Pesce spade di nostro mare!"

About the Author

Steven Tencati is a retired trial lawyer with a Bachelor's degree in history, a master's degree in history and a Juris Doctorate in law.

He was born in Massachusetts, and raised in California.

His grandparents hail from the opposite ends of Italy.

His grandparents on his mother's side are from
the south of Italy in Sicily;

His grandparents on his father's side are from
the north of Italy in Piedmont.

But for the blending of all Italians
in the North End of Boston, Massachusetts,

His parents would never have met.

Steven now resides in Edmonds, Washington
with his wife of 41 years.